▶ Reading Gandhi in the Twenty-First Century

DOI: 10.1057/978-1-137-32516-7

## Other Palgrave Pivot titles

Maria-Ionela Neagu: Decoding Political Discourse: Conceptual Metaphors and Argumentation

Ralf Emmers: Resource Management and Contested Territories in East Asia

Peter Conn: Adoption: A Brief Social and Cultural History

Joel Gwynne: Erotic Memoirs and Postfeminism: The Politics of Pleasure

Ira Nadel: Modernism's Second Act: A Cultural Narrative

Andy Sumner and Richard Mallett: The Future of Foreign Aid: Development Cooperation and the New Geography of Global Poverty

Tariq Mukhimer: Hamas Rule in Gaza: Human Rights under Constraint

Khen Lampert: Meritocratic Education and Social Worthlessness

G. Douglas Atkins: Swift's Satires on Modernism: Battlegrounds of Reading and Writing

David Schultz: American Politics in the Age of Ignorance: Why Lawmakers Choose Belief over Research

G. Douglas Atkins: T.S. Eliot Materialized: Literal Meaning and Embodied Truth

Martin Barker: Live To Your Local Cinema: The Remarkable Rise of Livecasting

Michael Bennett: Narrating the Past through Theatre: Four Crucial Texts

Arthur Asa Berger: Media, Myth, and Society

Hamid Dabashi: Being a Muslim in the World

David Elliott: Fukushima: Impacts and Implications

Milton J. Esman: The Emerging American Garrison State

Kelly Forrest: Moments, Attachment and Formations of Selfhood: Dancing with Now

Steve Fuller: Preparing for Life in Humanity 2.0

Ioannis N. Grigoriadis: Instilling Religion in Greek and Turkish Nationalism: A "Sacred Synthesis"

Jonathan Hart: Textual Imitation: Making and Seeing in Literature

Akira Iriye: Global and Transnational History: The Past, Present, and Future

Mikael Klintman: Citizen-Consumers and Evolutionary Theory: Reducing Environmental Harm through Our Social Motivation

Helen Jefferson Lenskyj: Gender Politics and the Olympic Industry

Christos Lynteris: The Spirit of Selflessness in Maoist China: Socialist Medicine and the New Man

Ekpen James Omonbude: Cross-border Oil and Gas Pipelines and the Role of the Transit Country: Economics, Challenges, and Solutions

William F. Pinar: Curriculum Studies in the United States: Present Circumstances, Intellectual Histories

Henry Rosemont, Jr.: A Reader's Companion to the Confucian Analects

Kazuhiko Togo (editor): Japan and Reconciliation in Post-war Asia: The Murayama Statement and Its Implications

Joel Wainwright: Geopiracy: Oaxaca, Militant Empiricism, and Geographical Thought

Kath Woodward: Sporting Times

DOI: 10.1057/978-1-137-32516-7

palgrave▶pivot

# Reading Gandhi in the Twenty-First Century

Niranjan Ramakrishnan

DOI: 10.1057/978-1-137-32516-7

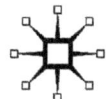

READING GANDHI IN THE TWENTY-FIRST CENTURY
Copyright © Niranjan Ramakrishnan, 2013.

First published in 2013 by
PALGRAVE MACMILLAN®
in the United States—a division of St. Martin's Press LLC,
175 Fifth Avenue, New York, NY 10010.

Where this book is distributed in the UK, Europe and the rest of the world,
this is by Palgrave Macmillan, a division of Macmillan Publishers Limited,
registered in England, company number 785998, of Houndmills, Basingstoke,
Hampshire RG21 6XS.

Palgrave Macmillan is the global academic imprint of the above companies and
has companies and representatives throughout the world.

Palgrave® and Macmillan® are registered trademarks in the United States,
the United Kingdom, Europe and other countries.

ISBN: 978–1–137–32516–7 EPUB
ISBN: 978–1–137–32515–0 PDF
ISBN: 978–1–137–32514–3 Hardback

Library of Congress Cataloging-in-Publication Data is available from the
Library of Congress.

A catalogue record of the book is available from the British Library.

First edition: 2013

www.palgrave.com/pivot

DOI: 10.1057/9781137325150

*To*
*the memory of my father, K. G. Ramakrishnan,*
*who taught me about Gandhi,*
*and*
*to my sister Nitya,*
*who lives my father's favorite Gandhi line:*
*"Fearlessness is the first requisite of spirituality."*

DOI: 10.1057/978-1-137-32516-7

# Contents

Acknowledgments      viii

Prologue: A World at Sea      1

1   What's So Great about Gandhi, Anyway?      7

2   Gandhi in the Time of Terrorism      13

3   Privatization...Privation...Privacy      25

4   Globalization...of What?      35

5   A Fundamental(ist) Irony      43

6   Environmentalism      48

7   The C(l)ash of Civilizations      55

8   East versus West: Win, Lose or Draw?      65

9   Media Matters...*and Citizen Mutters*      75

10   Technological Titans, Moral Midgets: The Death of Aleksandr Solzhenitsyn      85

11   Corruption and Its Discontents      90

DOI: 10.1057/978-1-137-32516-7

12   Of Suicides and Stock Markets:
*Leave It to Psainath*                                         94

13   Unbroken Connectivity, Brokered Lives:
Industrialism and Its Consequences                          100

14   W(h)ither the State?                                     109

Epilogue: Where Do We Go from Here?                          121

Bibliography                                                  132

Index                                                         134

DOI: 10.1057/978-1-137-32516-7

# Acknowledgments

Mahatma Gandhi declared long ago that he had never copyrighted any of his writings. Nonetheless, I am thankful to the Publications Division, Government of India, for its *Collected Works of Mahatma Gandhi*, from which most of the Gandhi quotations in this book are taken. I also thank the website www.gandhiserve.org for its efforts in providing the *Collected Works* in a conveniently searchable PDF format.

For close to a decade now, Jeffrey St. Clair has published most of my pieces in the inimitable *Counterpunch*, the brainchild of Jeff and that recently departed genius of Anglo-American journalism Alexander Cockburn. I have drawn on several of my *Counterpunch* pieces in this book.

It has been my good fortune to have my work carried frequently on the online pages of Binu Matthew's doughty effort, *Countercurrents*. Chapter 12, "Of Suicides and Stock Markets," is an expansion of one such contribution.

In 2008 the *Oregonian* newspaper gave me an opportunity to serve as a community writer, and featured a series of my columns on its website. I've taken the liberty of drawing on some of those writings in this book.

Many thanks to Paul Craig Roberts, Aakar Patel, Andrew Bacevich, P. Sainath, Michael Nagler, Sampad Mahapatra, and Morris Berman for permission to quote from their writings.

Shortly before his untimely death, Joe Bageant gave me blanket permission to use any of his writings. I have quoted from one of his pieces on the assumption that ornery as he

DOI: 10.1057/978-1-137-32516-7

claimed to be, he would not go to the extent of rescinding this liberality once he got to the other world.

Other sources quoted in this book have been acknowledged in the chapter endnotes.

Isabella Yeager at Palgrave Macmillan has been a pleasure to work with. Earlier, Farideh Koohi-Kamali and Sarah Nathan were equally responsive and courteous. Vidhya Jayaprakash at Newgen has been utterly professional, her unnamed copy editor colleague simply superb.

Sapna Rahim and Latha Nair came through with their timely help.

On a personal level, there are many people to thank for their support, direct or indirect, in making this book a reality. My wife and children have been constant companions in an ongoing struggle. My mother and aunts have prayed for my recovery from afar, my mother-in-law has shipped me innumerable care packages of her delicious health snacks. My friends in the Daftar Group have been indefatigable in their generosity. Ken and Marianne Nielsen, Martha Worley, Betty Parker, and Patricia Saier and her family have all been pillars to lean on in Portland. In Hyderabad, Kumar and Radhika, Kishore, Prateek, Akhil, Shobha and Vasu, Srinivas and Madhavi, Uma, Shankar, Kiran, and the ever-smiling Sindhu have all gone far beyond any call of duty or reason in making my health their priority. The solicitude of one and all at the Carnival Club will always be a pleasant memory. "Railway" Anand's resourcefulness, Sujata's daily inquiries, Sucharita's constant encouragement, Jayanthi's cheerful supply runs, Ashwin's humor, the Cheela-Rao exhanges and Vijji Chitti's repartee are all testimony to the therapeutic nature of a bevy of loving relatives. Of friends too – Arundhati's visits laden with gifts of Gandhi books will ever be etched in my mind; the affection and concern of long-lost MEA school classmates including Meenakshi, Janardhan, Jayaraman, Hari, Nanu, Santhanam, Vichu, Uma, Chuppini, Cheeru, VL, SV, Rajagopal, and Crangi has been overwhelming. Likewise former colleagues Vinay and Ukil. My sister Nitya has been a powerhouse of organization and compassion, making it all possible. Her son Anushrut is a chip off the old block. Pandit my attendant is a gem, as are the exercise crew of Durga, Rehman, and Nizam in Hyderabad; their Delhi counterparts Vijender the Great, Raju, Sachin, Kapil, Sunil, Vishal, and Shoaib have all been outstanding. From the ministrations of Prasanna the "ideological" physiotherapist both my muscle tone and my Telugu have benefited, though perhaps not equally.

DOI: 10.1057/978-1-137-32516-7

palgrave▸**pivot**

www.palgrave.com/pivot

# Prologue: A World at Sea

It was probably Alvin Toffler who first suggested the source of our discomfort with change. He noted that it was not change itself but rather its increasing speed that troubled us—which is to say, we are unnerved not so much by the velocity as by the acceleration.

To observe that the past two decades have turned the world upside down would be to state the obvious. Be it a farmer in India or a store manager in China, a mid-level executive in the American Midwest or a former party commissar in the former Soviet Union, the lives of all have been affected, often drastically. That the pace of these years may have proved kind to some and harsh to others is a separate matter. The point is that the impact has been deep and widespread, sparing no one, whether or not they sought it.

Toffler's *Future Shock* came out in the 1970s, and his observation about change growing ever-faster has proven entirely true. Many would point to the increased speed of communication and large-scale human migrations as examples; the Internet would be high on most people's lists. The rapidity of change has pushed other futurists to enhance their own visualizations of what else might be expected in the decades to come, on the basis of the frequency of technological surges, new materials, and altered lifestyles.

Less evident is any widespread manifestation of the second aspect of Toffler's prediction: a concomitant angst and disquiet on account of change. Though the person on the street might speak wistfully of simpler times and shake his head at their passing, he continues firmer than ever with his faith in technology, the chief agent of change. Remedies for chronic diseases, prospects of endless food and entertainment, underwritten by bioengineering miracles for limitless energy and pervasive connectivity, are givens in this unfolding technological Panglossia. Those of a more ethereal disposition see in the increased human interaction and diversity made practicable by fast communication and transportation a way toward unprecedented world harmony.

Paradoxically, even those who inveigh against the ill-effects of modernity, if not industrialization per se, prescribe solutions that envision even more technology, only they might call it "smarter." The environmental movement might boast of recent Nobel prizes and growing numbers of celebrities going "green," but the overall trend is definitely toward greater reliance on technology and technology-based consumption, not less.[1] It is the faith of both the world's elites and its middle classes that science is the answer, that technology is the future, that gadgetry will resolve humanity's problems.

It is a premise this book seeks to examine. It does so in the context of a previous book, the work of a futurist from a hundred years ago. Everyone has heard of its author, but few would think of him as a futurist. Indeed, many might view him as the very antithesis of one; even in his own time he was regarded as rather a throwback to an even earlier age.

Nonetheless, I believe Mahatma Gandhi was a futurist in the best sense of the word. He foresaw trends and had the confidence to record his predictions and prescriptions in bold and stark terms. He did so, not in a stray article or opinion piece, but over a lifetime of speeches, writings—and living—beginning with *Hind Swaraj*, the remarkable book he started writing in 1909 (and completed in 1910).[2]

The essential mark of a futurist is the ability to visualize something that does not exist; it is merely an added bonus if he happens to get it right. A hundred years later, however, as this book hopes to show, each passing week appears to bear out the strength of Gandhi's prognostications.

But the context in which he made them is equally worthy of attention.

Toffler's thesis notwithstanding, change—and even its rapidity—are not wholly new. The Industrial Revolution and its offshoots have been altering the world almost continually over the past two centuries. Even as we in our day pride ourselves on being *the* "science" people, we are merely nurturing a fond notion our forefathers too cherished. Each generation in the recent past has been united by its illusion that it alone,

DOI: 10.1057/978-1-137-32516-7

ever more than its predecessors, is privy to the scientific outlook. It is sobering to note that belief in the gods of science and technology has been with us far longer than our own lifetimes: indeed, they were as much watchwords in the first decades of the twentieth century as they are in the twenty-first.

While Gandhi was writing *Hind Swaraj*, Europe was thrilling to the sounds of the airplane and the automobile. The telephone and the telegraph were already several decades old. The electric light was spreading into the streets, replacing gas lamps. A Wi-Fi connection on a plane may be a big deal to us today, but can we declare it was any less exciting suddenly to be able to cross the ocean in a few hours or light up entire cities at dusk?

If anything, the early twentieth century was a time of singular hope and belief in technology. The flaws and ill-effects of industrial progress were less manifest, and it was the chassis upon which the juggernaut of Western civilization rested as it hurtled to the far ends of the earth. Hilaire Belloc captured this central truth in its crassest form:

> *Whatever happens,*
>
> *We have got*
>
> *The Maxim Gun*
>
> *And they have not.*[3]

For all the arguments for Western civilization and its claims of moral, political, and cultural ascendancy over the colonial world, the most essential element of superiority lay in science, with military might its clearest exposition. Around the same time, another Englishman wrote something showing he too had grasped this seminal fact through first-hand experience. Writing about the River War, in which he had fought the Sudanese dervishes, Winston Churchill noted, "and were it not that Christianity is sheltered in the strong arms of science, the science against which it had vainly struggled, the civilisation of modern Europe might fall, as fell the civilisation of ancient Rome."[4]

But even this was only the tip of the iceberg. Along with the science and the guns came an industrial organization and an incipient management and communication culture that combined to achieve a magical efficiency that the "lesser breeds" of the planet could only behold in awe. India and China might hark back to their ancient monuments or keep pointing to their inventions of the zero and gunpowder, but everyone

DOI: 10.1057/978-1-137-32516-7

at the start of the twentieth century—in East and West—knew in their hearts where the future lay.

Thus, in 1909 Western civilization was the unquestioned beacon of the world. We must recall that this was before Europe had blown itself to smithereens in a four-year orgy that would start shortly. If the European powers came out of that holocaust with all their colonies intact, albeit in different hands, one can only imagine the feeling prior to this exhaustion. The writing on the wall was clear: the European path was the way of the future, against which any cultural struggle would be futile, if not imbecilic.

It was in this setting, on a ship back to South Africa from England after meeting with the top rung of English politicians and having seen British power at its height, that Gandhi wrote a tract debunking the entire notion of Western civilization. The themes of the book would stay with him and inform his thinking throughout the rest of his life, although he was keenly aware of the attraction the Western model held for so many of his compatriots who thought it was the quickest way to a better life.[5]

The world knows Gandhi only for his leadership of India's freedom struggle. He has been enshrined for his devotion to peaceful means, a fact that unfortunately endears his example to every oppressor who fears a violent revolt. It is the fate of multifaceted individuals to be known mainly for just one or two things. Gandhi's tragedy is that he is unsung, even unknown, for his greatest contribution, even in the land of his birth. This is a real tragedy, for what he identified in *Hind Swaraj* was a fatal flaw that would make the twentieth century the bloodiest in history, and set the twenty-first up for ecological catastrophe.

Gandhi was also one of the earliest environmentalists, but from a spiritual viewpoint, not a scientific one. He would not have known technical terms such as "rainforest diversity" or "population load," but he understood better than most the implications for both humankind and life at large of unfettered human greed.

Mark Twain quipped that it was dangerous to make predictions, especially about the future. One might add, "even more so when every trend is contrary to your thesis." But this is exactly what Gandhi did. When he began writing *Hind Swaraj* in 1909, he faced a West that was resplendent, confident, on top of the world. Even when he died some forty years later, the Europe of 1909 was in shambles but the European model was intact; indeed, it was gaining adherents in newer places still. Every country in

DOI: 10.1057/978-1-137-32516-7

the East (and West) continued to pursue the Holy Grail of industrial expansion. India itself rejected Gandhi in its post-independence economic policies.

But sixty years after Gandhi's assassination, on the centenary of *Hind Swaraj*, it is Gandhi who seems prophetic. The Western path appears to have reached its end. The collective flailing of the world's political and business elites during the years since proclaiming a global economic crisis in 2008 is practically a QED for *Hind Swaraj*, and there is something almost poetic about the meltdown coinciding with its centenary. The book is a repudiation of every economic dictum of a globalized industrial economy. To me, it has always seemed the work most congruent with Gandhi's own striving toward liberation, not merely from foreign rule but from all thralldom. In his own words, "I am not interested in freeing India merely from the English yoke. I am bent upon freeing India from any yoke whatsoever."[6]

How do major issues of our time relate to what Gandhi set down in *Hind Swaraj* and his later writings? From the angle of expanding freedom in particular, where do we stand a hundred years after *Hind Swaraj*?

My effort in this book is to seek some understanding of these two questions through the fourteen essays, this prologue, and an epilogue. That my contents list covers a rather wide swath of topics is a fair charge, but it is no exaggeration to reply that Gandhi had strong views on almost all of them. Over a lifetime of journalism and correspondence, Gandhi had things to say about many issues, and did so even while admitting freely the possibility of internal contradiction. Echoing Emerson, he declared that he had never tried to be consistent but rather to speak the truth as it appeared to him at the moment.[7] The result, as he put it, was that he had grown "from truth to truth." Within almost one hundred volumes[8] of freewheeling expression, though, there is an "essential Gandhi" to be discerned. It has been my effort here to interpret his words and actions in the context of the issues we face today. And if any single text of Gandhi's writings can be said to represent the "essential Gandhi," *Hind Swaraj*, I think, would come closest.

## Notes

1 Nor are such lines of reasoning unique to ecology: during the past couple of election seasons in America many politicians argued that in George W.

DOI: 10.1057/978-1-137-32516-7

Bush's place, they would have fought a smarter war in Iraq. Or in Afghanistan instead.

2   Gandhi wrote *Hind Swaraj* on board the *SS Kildonan Castle* during his voyage back to South Africa from England. Writing furiously in longhand, he had to pen half the book with his left hand after having tired out his right.

3   Hilaire Belloc, "The Modern Traveller," (London; E. Arnold, 1898).

4   *The River War*, first edition, Vol. II, pp. 248–250 (London: Longmans, Green & Co., 1899).

5   Or in more recent times, to the good life.

6   *Young India*, June 12, 1924. *Collected Works of Mahatma Gandhi*, Vol. 28 p.137.

7   "At the time of writing I never think of what I have said before. My aim is not to be consistent with my previous statements on a given question, but to be consistent with truth as it may present itself to me at a given moment. The result has been that I have grown from truth to truth" (*Collected Works of Mahatma Gandhi*, Vol. 76, p. 356).

8   *Collected Works of Mahatma Gandhi*, Publications Division, Government of India, 1999, 98 volumes.

DOI: 10.1057/978-1-137-32516-7

# 1
# What's So Great about Gandhi, Anyway?

Abstract: *What sets Gandhi apart? Did he think differently, did he act differently, or was he just a pious man who happened to be in the right place at the right time? Chapter 1 offers a brief examination of his approach to a variety of issues, such as terrorism, freedom, economic policy, industrialism, technology, etc.*

Ramakrishnan, Niranjan. *Reading Gandhi in the Twenty-First Century*. New York: Palgrave Macmillan, 2013.
DOI: 10.1057/9781137325150.

"Mahatma Gandhi was OK, but he was no Manmohan Singh," remarked a friend of mine. I laughed out loud at this deadpan humor, only to realize that my friend, a smart and successful technology baron in Silicon Valley, was serious. He genuinely thought that Gandhi's contribution was merely to freeing the country from the British, and that Singh, who as Indian finance minister had *freed the Indian economy from governmental shackles* in the early 1990s, thus ushering India into the global economy, was clearly the larger figure.

This is a notion shared by increasing numbers of the intelligentsia, both in India and abroad. To many, Gandhi is no more than a goody-goody icon who talked about nonviolence and held Luddite views on industry and trade. True, he may have been honest and upright, but then those were different times. Some (mistakenly, in my opinion) associate Gandhi with India's pursuit of economic protectionism after independence (a policy followed by his associate Jawaharlal Nehru) and hold Gandhi responsible for India's perceived backwardness. Others consider his approach to Muslims and Pakistan naive and gullible. All in all, they conclude, the coward who shot him in 1948 did India a favor, for Gandhi would have been an albatross around our modern necks. In a world where terrorism lurks at every corner and smartphones sit in every pocket, Gandhi is passé.

Is he?

As I watch world events unfold, Gandhi's life appears increasingly relevant. With each passing day, his words and methods seem even more uncannily prescient.

Gandhi had numerous interesting and formidable personal characteristics—prodigious courage both physical and political, enormous self-discipline, asceticism and industry (more than a hundred volumes of writings and twenty-hour days), a fine sense of humor, and the ability to laugh at himself—that must have played a major role in the making of the Mahatma. But if I were to condense his political philosophy into one phrase, it would be this: the freedom of the individual.

Complete liberty, for Gandhi, was the first and last goal. India's freedom from Britain, to him, was only an objective along the path, and a rather insignificant one at that. Far more important was the ability of each individual to seek out his or her own freedom. "Real Swaraj [freedom] will come, not by the acquisition of authority by a few, but by the acquisition of the capacity by all to resist authority when abused,"

DOI: 10.1057/978-1-137-32516-7

he wrote.[1] I think of this statement every time I recall how mutely the public of the United States accepted the slap delivered full to its face by the Rehnquist Supreme Court after the 2000 presidential elections, followed by the post-9/11 march of official arbitrariness and open violation of liberties.

It is also in the context of liberty that *ahimsa*, Gandhi's creed of nonviolence, must be understood. It was not out of some sense of piety that he espoused peaceful means. He held nonviolence to be essential because it afforded the only democratic means of struggle. It was available to everyone—not just to those who owned weapons. Second, a violent victory, even a just one, would prove only that violence had triumphed, not necessarily that justice had done so. A violent solution would mean that the fate of the unarmed many would be mortgaged to the benevolence of the armed few. This was contrary to liberty as Gandhi saw it.

An extremely intelligent man, he had a knack of cutting right through shibboleths to the heart of the matter. In an earlier echo of the American position on Iraq and Afghanistan, the British kept telling India that they would leave India in a heartbeat, if only they could be sure the country would not fall into anarchy. This made some sense to many in view of the vicissitudes and general caprice of feudal rule in pre-British India, until Gandhi gently reminded us that good governance was no substitute for self-governance. When one hears the cant that passes for political discussion on our airwaves, how one longs for a similar voice today.

Gandhi saw that millions had lost their livelihood because the British, in a former era of globalization, had systematically destroyed India's cottage industries to create a market for the products of the Industrial Revolution. Gandhi was the chief architect of India's revived cottage industry. Although this was a magnificent achievement in itself, even more telling was the way he brought it about. He did not run complaining to the British government, asking it to reduce exports to India. Instead, he mobilized people to buy Indian-made goods. Huge bonfires of foreign cloth resulted in the handspun Indian fabric *khadi* replacing foreign mill-cloth to become, in Jawaharlal Nehru's words, "the livery of India's freedom."

This too has to do with freedom. To have demanded something of the government would only have increased its power. Gandhi instead chose to empower each individual to make a statement by shedding foreign cloth and wearing *khadi*. Today, a third rail of American politics is the

DOI: 10.1057/978-1-137-32516-7

word "trade." It is commonly accepted, and rarely challenged, that trade is a deity to be propitiated at all costs—even if doing so means sacrificing jobs, families, homes, even towns or entire ecologies. Gandhi wrote that he would like to see all of a community's needs met from within a reasonable radius. Some years ago *Vegetarian Times* carried a mind-boggling statistic: the average item consumed in America travels 1,200 miles. Is it any surprise we have to invade other countries for oil? As American gadflies such as Ralph Nader and Pat Buchanan rail against NAFTA and the WTO, one wonders why they haven't thought of organizing a movement to buy American-made products.

Gandhi was an exponent of "demand-side economics." This was a much longer and more arduous path than supply-side economics, but a more enduring one, and one with fewer deleterious side-effects. He believed that, ultimately, the only guarantee of good society lay in the quality of the citizenry. Benjamin Franklin's famous reply upon being asked whether the United States had a republic or a monarchy—"A republic, if you can keep it"—approximates Gandhi's belief. A society with no demand for cigarettes, for instance, would soon stop manufacturing them. Gandhi believed the gift of liberty carried with it the utmost moral responsibility for its use. In a famous interview with the noted birth-control proponent Margaret Sanger, he said flat out that he was against contraception, as it meant escaping the consequences of one's action. He was no politically correct weathervane, preferring rather the liberty to say what he thought. He gave Sanger an analogy along these lines (not an exact quote): "I overeat, and instead of suffering the consequences of my indulgence, I go to the doctor and get some pills. To mitigate the side-effects of the pills, I then take some whiskey.... Where does it end?"[2] He would certainly be aghast at the blithe acceptance of abortion today. He always connected individual morality and public policy.

Consider the drug war, for example. We do practically nothing to discourage the taking of drugs. Instead, we pour money into drug interdiction efforts, change foreign governments, denude entire countrysides, and fight endlessly (Panama, Colombia, Peru) because we don't have the guts to demand the highest of our own citizenry. Gandhi was unafraid of public opprobrium, even assassination. Every politician is willing to tell us what is wrong with someone else; Gandhi was different because he told us what was wrong with us. "Let us turn the searchlight inward,"

DOI: 10.1057/978-1-137-32516-7

he once said, to the astonishment of a crowd that had gathered to hear some rousing rhetoric condemning the British, only to find him spouting uncomfortable home truths about how Indians themselves enabled British rule in a hundred small ways.

If we turn the searchlight upon our own contradictions, we might wonder how, while complaining about the disappearance of our forests, we continue to build new housing developments (and prize this as an index of economic health), or how, while complaining of rising medical costs, we cannot stay away from our Big Macs.

Like Jefferson, Gandhi believed in small government, noting with approval the saying "That government is best which governs least." Once again, this is an offshoot of his ideal of least external control, and maximum individual freedom, coupled with complete moral responsibility—making for an uncharacteristic meeting point between Karl Marx (the state withering away) and Ayn Rand (individual freedom from the collective). As fear-stricken citizens throughout the world surrender their personal rights, in the name of safeguarding their personal security, to their fear-stricken governments, which in turn surrender their sovereignty to faceless agencies such as the WTO in the name of economic security, we might recall Gandhi's words "Fearlessness is the first requisite of spirituality. Cowards can never be moral."[3]

The art of forging popular movements based on inveterate opposition to injustice, while always demanding the highest moral standards both of the individual and of the collective, is Gandhi's enduring contribution to politics. It is almost certainly due to Gandhi's movement that India, for all its flaws, has remained a liberal democracy. (No other country freed from the colonial yoke can make a similar claim.) Without a Gandhi, India might well have ended up like Pakistan, a hotbed of intolerance and obscurantism. (It might be pure coincidence that the more India rejects Gandhi, the more that seems to be the direction in which it is headed.) At the risk of oversimplification, we can note that Martin Luther King applied Gandhi's means and managed to avoid a West Bank in America. The Palestinians did not—and did not.

Some time ago, the Indian socialist Rammanohar Lohia wrote that the twentieth century had produced one innovation, the atom bomb, and one innovator, Mahatma Gandhi. As paranoia and insanity sweep our times, Lohia's terms come into sharper focus: fear versus freedom. In this consequential contest, Gandhi is not merely relevant; he is central.

DOI: 10.1057/978-1-137-32516-7

# Notes

1  *Young India*, January 29,1925. *Collected Works of Mahatma Gandhi*, Vol. 30, p. 159.
2  "You do not take chocolate for the sake of your physical need. You take it for pleasure and then ask the doctor for an antidote. Perhaps you tell the doctor that whiskey befogs your brain and he gives you an antidote." Interview with Margaret Sanger, 1935. *Collected Works of Mahatma Gandhi*, Vol. 68, p. 192.
3  *Collected Works of Mahatma Gandhi*, Vol. 24, p. 411.

DOI: 10.1057/978-1-137-32516-7

# 2
## Gandhi in the Time of Terrorism

**Abstract:** *Since 9/11, terrorism has come to occupy center stage in twenty-first-century political discourse. Yet the problem long precedes some planes hitting two tall buildings on a bright autumn morning. Gandhi not only was aware of the problem but even wrote about it, using the very word. What self-deceptions about terrorism are we prey to, and how can Gandhi help us resolve this endless war on ourselves?*

Ramakrishnan, Niranjan. *Reading Gandhi in the Twenty-First Century.* New York: Palgrave Macmillan, 2013. DOI: 10.1057/9781137325150.

"Happy families are all alike," Tolstoy writes in *Anna Karenina*. "Every unhappy family is unhappy in its own way."

The latter statement seems much the norm in the case of terrorism. From Russia to Australia, from Iran to Japan, from Great Britain to Argentina, not to mention the United States of America, every land can relate its own "favorite" incident of firebombing, kidnapping, hijacking, or other innovations in mayhem attempted or successful. Add assassination to the list and you might need a microscope to find an entity on the world map that can claim to have been terror-free.

Little surprise, then, that the word "terrorism" lights up the radar screens in every context; practically everyone can associate themselves with some place that has been hit by terror. For the philosophically inclined, it might be tempting to recall the parable in which the Buddha, beseeched by a woman to revive her dead child, assures her he would do so—if only she could procure a handful of rice from a home where no death has ever occurred.

Should we similarly console ourselves that terror, like death and taxes, is inevitable? Most people, at least in places where terror has not (yet?) become the norm, would say no. Everyone accepts death as natural, but we hold terror to be an aberration, a fear that seems different from other varieties of fear.

What distinguishes *terror* from good old everyday *fear*? I haven't looked up the dictionary meaning of either word before writing this, but most people would agree there is a difference in meaning as both words are commonly used. Everyone has fears. We fear injury, death, illness. We might fear losing a job or forfeiting our home, or for the health of a friend or relative. Then there are specialized fears—phobias about spiders, spaces, heights, etc.—a long list. But we don't associate the word "terror" with any of these. Even though we use "terrified," or "terrorized," as a synonym for "fear," "terrorism" seems to be in a different league altogether.

So what is terror? Below are some aspects to consider:

1  *Terror has a face*: "Terror" strikes fear, of course. But it does more. It seems terror has elements of the macabre, the unexpected, an active component of malice. Terror has personification. The key aspect of the terrorist act is that it is meant to be remembered, to serve as a warning or a calling card, a self-propagating organism.

2  *Terror is collective*: There is another discernible pattern in the usage of the two words. Although an average kidnapper may strike fear

DOI: 10.1057/978-1-137-32516-7

into the heart of a captive and the water-boarder terrify his detainee, we do not automatically think of these as terrorist acts. In common parlance, terror always seems to be characterized by a collective fear. In fact, the ability to induce fear in a large section of the populace seems an essential facet of terror. Hitler's Blitzkrieg, General Dyer's iron fist in the Punjab in 1919, and Lenin's attitude to his "class enemies" all meet this criterion.

3 *Terror is about the future*: It is accurate to say that terror requires an active and sentient agency that outlives the act. In its absence even a collective calamity induces only fear, not terror. Hurricane Katrina was fearsome for all affected by its ravages, but no one would have confused it with terrorism.

4 *Terror seeks to modify average behavior*: Related to the items 2 and 3 above, the terrorist aims to send a "copy to all" message. The immediate damage caused by the terrorist act, its *effect*, is often less important than its *affect*: causing the public at large to modify their behavior. Every dictator who usurps power, after killing or locking up opponents, declares that those who are "law abiding" have nothing to fear. What this means, though, is that anyone who dares say anything against the dictator has much to worry about.

5 *Terror banishes rationality*: The final aspect of terror is the suspension of rationality it engenders. Fear is something we can consider rationally, while terror induces a wholesale irrationality. It could well be that what is (merely) fearsome to one may be terrifying to another, and vice versa. Part of the rationality that terror dissipates is the ability to take a dispassionate view of terror itself.

This last item is possibly the most important element of terror. Unless it causes a self-propagating irrationality, we may argue that even if the other elements are present, an outrage really does not succeed as a terrorist act. In an article published some years ago I termed 9/11 a black hole that has sucked any sense of balance out of all subsequent national discourse in America. The brave and brilliant libertarian commentator Justin Raimondo goes further, calling the complete inversion of reality in America following the 9/11 terrorist attacks a descent into an alternate-dimension Bizarro World:

> This, I believe, is proof positive of what I call the Bizarro Effect, a direct result of the 9/11 terrorist attacks. What happened was this: the sheer force of the explosion as those planes hit the World Trade Center and slammed

DOI: 10.1057/978-1-137-32516-7

into the Pentagon forced us into an alternate dimension where up is down, news is entertainment, and a rational critique of U.S. foreign policy is considered sheer amusement. Here in Bizarro World, everything is upended: not only our morals, but our grasp of reality, and, indeed, the concept of reality itself.[1]

In one sense, as we shall see shortly, Raimondo is echoing Gandhi: the terrorist's success or failure lies largely in our hands, in how we respond to a terrorist act, no matter how dastardly.

## Civilians and combatants

If inflicting a loss of reason is the sweetest prize for a terrorist, one of the surest signs of vanishing rationality is a catchphrase frequently heard in descriptions and discussions of terror. This phrase, "innocent civilians," is far from innocent. It raises the questions "Does that mean there are 'non-innocent' civilians as well? Are they eligible to be dispatched through terror, then, without regret? And what of non-civilians? Is their killing OK?" When American politicians speak of the 9/11 terrorists murdering 3,000 of "our innocent civilians" in cold blood in the Twin Towers, I wonder whether they realize they are tacitly exempting the attack that same day on the Pentagon, a military target.

No less fatuous are many spokesmen from the Muslim world. We've heard statements from them such as "Islam forbids the killing of innocents," or even "Islam forbids the killing of Muslims." Anxious to buttress the case that theirs has ever been a faith of "tender ruth" (to borrow from Kipling's "Ballad of the King's Mercy"), some even argue that Islam from its earliest days always gave its captives the choice to convert (the alternative being death). One strains at the leash, as it were, seeking to scream at the TV, radio, or computer once more, asking whether if Islam said it was OK to kill this or that sect, would that make it fine?

Terror, as we see, may shatter many things. Rationality is only its first victim. Compassion often follows close behind. Why do both official spokespeople and their contradictors resort to terms such as "innocent civilians" and "True Muslims" instead of viewing any killing for what it is? Could it be because both know that only by defining events in such specific terms would they gain wiggle-room to escape indictment of their own side?

DOI: 10.1057/978-1-137-32516-7

# Modern views of terrorism

Any discussion of terrorism seems to alight on one of three broad avenues of argument, for which we can frame some characterizing phrases. One is the "terrorist-as-rodent" approach. The second is "much can be said on both sides", and the third, "intelligent defense."

## The terrorist as rodent

This approach takes the view that whatever the grievance, there is no excuse for terrorism. Terrorists must be shown no mercy. To protect the safety and well-being of its citizens the state is justified in taking any and all steps to combat the scourge of terrorism and to treat terrorists as the vermin they are.

At first glance this appears most likely to be the view of hardened military or police officers. But they are not the only ones with such an unrelenting attitude, nor even perhaps the ones wedded most strongly to it. This view is just as prevalent in ostensibly liberal and upper middle-class circles.

Leaving aside the tempting prospect of asking those who hold terrorism to be the greatest threat to society whether they consider it dangerous enough to risk their own lives and those of their children in fighting it, we can ask a simpler question: "Are you willing to pay higher taxes for this purpose?" The question is reminiscent of an exchange in Gandhi's book *Satyagraha in South Africa*. "We are prepared to follow you to the gallows," some enthusiastic volunteers exclaim. To which Gandhi replies, "Jail is enough for me." Recent experience from the self-proclaimed scourge of terrorism in the world, the United States of America, might be instructive. The middle classes have consistently voted for those who claim to be strongest in fighting terror, while remaining equally constant in voting against tax increases.

The apparent hypocrisy of their stand is only a minor aspect of this frequently unconscious middle-class perfidy. A larger and often overlooked element is their readiness, in their current moment of fear, to yield a wide swath of hard-won or felicitously gifted protections against official arbitrariness. Experience shows that such expediencies rarely make their way out of the statute book even decades after the situation that purportedly made them so essential has long vanished.[2]

DOI: 10.1057/978-1-137-32516-7

## Much can be said on both sides

Another common response, frequently aired in drawing rooms far away from the strife, is that there are valid arguments to be made from both the terrorist and the official angles. As indeed there are, sometimes. People in areas suffering from terrorism (both the insurgent and the government variety), unfortunately, do not have the luxury of such an expansive perspective. At one time they might be relieved at being defended against an oppressive officialdom. At another time the same people might find their homes and resources (and sons) requisitioned at gunpoint for use against the same officialdom.

## Intelligent defense

When drawing-room equivocation becomes palpably effete and a muscular no-holds-barred military suppression has merely resulted in protracted mayhem and the sullying of the military force with charges of corruption and moral lapses, the stage is set for the proponents of "intelligent defense."

Wise men and women, often in a new incarnation of the "much can be said on both sides" argument, now begin to inform the public that "winning the hearts and minds" of the populace is key to success. To this end, nothing attracts like the mantra of "development." The region, they proclaim, is restive because it is underdeveloped. A mildly sinister subtext in this strategy is the hope to coopt a segment of the disaffected via blandishments. The lesson that history offers little to suggest that such bribery promotes anything but more disaffection, is always forgotten. Budgets are allocated, monies are sanctioned, and "nation-building" commences in earnest, paving the way for pipelines of ill-gotten wealth that empty into civilian pockets, rivaling the ones that previously drained into the defense complex.

Given the apparent universality of terror, and given its unique and insidious hallmarks, how should modern society deal with terror? Odd as it may sound, Mahatma Gandhi had a clue.

# Gandhi and terrorism

Gandhi was conversant with terrorism, even in ways it is practiced today. A hundred years ago, terrorism was a going proposition. This statement

DOI: 10.1057/978-1-137-32516-7

might seem distorted, and it requires some explanation. Certainly, there were no networks as powerful as a LeT or a Shining Path or an Al-Qaeda. Terrorist organizations were often just a handful of student idealists scrounging about for a firearm or a bomb. Nevertheless, considering that the state too was far less powerful and intrusive than it is today, the balance of forces between the two was unlikely to be too skewed. The sole difference was this: a hundred years ago states were not open sponsors of terrorism.[3] However, since Gandhi tended to view the state as a form of congealed violence, the lack of such overt involvement would have had little impact on his basic view of the matter.

In fact, Gandhi often referred to terror and terrorism in his writings— of the state, and of its opponents. But he was not terrorized by either. And he was never confused on a question that stymies every politician in our time: "How can one condemn terrorism while defending its practice by one's own side?" Gandhi escaped this problem because of his somewhat integrated (undifferentiated, to some of his critics) view of life, religion, politics, and economics. His approach to terrorism rested on a principle that was a cornerstone of his overall philosophy. He had thus no need to get into absurd dialectical or teleological contortions to suit the situation *du jour*. He simply stuck to the base note that from bad deeds could come no lasting good. His onetime disciple Rammanohar Lohia called it the principle of immediacy, namely that both one's current and long-term purposes (and actions) should stand scrutiny; there was no question of acquiescing in short-term evil in the name of some avowed "long-term benefit." There was also no question of arguing that "they did it first," the moral (and public relations) hazard of many a popular movement.

Gandhi's forgiveness of his assailants, both Indian and European, in South Africa may seem to his critics an easy choice for a rising public figure who could only accrue greater acclaim through such magnanimity. But in time Gandhi would get caught in a moral dilemma worthy of Raju, the hero in *Guide*.[4] The year was 1931. A serious test of Gandhi's stance against violence came at the time of Bhagat Singh's execution. A young man of twenty-three, Bhagat Singh was a national hero both for his anti–British activities and for the great courage and stoic dignity he displayed in the face of incredible hardships, including torture, during his imprisonment by the British. Admiration for this phenomenal young man was sky-high; he was soon an icon whose popularity in India during that era rivaled if not exceeded Gandhi's own.

DOI: 10.1057/978-1-137-32516-7

It was widely hoped in India that Gandhi would use his moral standing to successfully appeal against the young patriot's death sentence. However, while he did express hope that Bhagat Singh's life would be spared, he stopped short of making it a nonnegotiable issue, instead becoming philosophical, even a little circumlocutory, appealing to the government's sense of discretion, et cetera. Rather than condemning the government's decision outright, he talked of how some powers should be enjoyed in name only and not exercised. It was a huge blow to his street popularity when he refused to make the commutation of Bhagat Singh's death sentence a make-or-break issue in his ongoing negotiations with the Raj.

India was plunged into mourning with Bhagat Singh's hanging on March 23, 1931. About a week later Gandhi wrote in his journal a kind of explanation[5] for his much-maligned silence. It deserves to be quoted at length, for it throws light on his attitude to (even patriotic) violence and is of a piece with his statements on other acts of violence against British officials by Indian revolutionaries:

> Bhagat Singh and his two associates have been hanged. The Congress made many attempts to save their lives and the Government entertained many hopes of it, but all has been in vain.
>
> Bhagat Singh did not wish to live. He refused to apologize, or even file an appeal. Bhagat Singh was not a devotee of non-violence, but he did not subscribe to the religion of violence. He took to violence due to helplessness and to defend his homeland. In his last letter, Bhagat Singh wrote—"I have been arrested while waging a war. For me there can be no gallows. Put me into the mouth of a cannon and blow me off." These heroes had conquered the fear of death. Let us bow to them a thousand times for their heroism.
>
> But we should not imitate their act. In our land of millions of destitute and crippled people, if we take to the practice of seeking justice through murder, there will be a terrifying situation. Our poor people will become victims of our atrocities. By making a dharma of violence, we shall be reaping the fruit of our own actions.
>
> Hence, though we praise the courage of these brave men, we should never countenance their activities. Our dharma is to swallow our anger, abide by the discipline of non-violence and carry out our duty.[6]

This passage remains as much an example of Gandhi's political courage as Bhagat Singh's own attitude to the gallows represented the pinnacle of physical courage. Gandhi could criticize Bhagat Singh's violence with a

DOI: 10.1057/978-1-137-32516-7

free conscience only because he himself was equally ready to die for the country. Gandhi also realized that not every young idealist with a gun or a bomb had the moral fiber of a Bhagat Singh. He was anticipating the frequently misquoted version of Eric Hoffer's words: "Every 'great cause' begins as a Movement, becomes a Business, and eventually degenerates into a Racket."[7] That so many armed "revolutionary movements" have over time disintegrated into quasi-criminal mafias is a matter of record. Gandhi was clear in his mind that any equivocation on the matter of violence would undo much of what he had stood for over the decades.

The attitude expressed in the quotation above appears consistent with his stance nine years earlier, during the famous Chauri Chaura incident, when, at the height of his noncooperation movement, a group of protest-ers provoked by the police had turned violent and had burned down a police station where the outnumbered policemen had hidden.

Without even consulting with the Congress Working Committee, Gandhi called off the national civil disobedience movement which until then had been growing by leaps and bounds. He took personal respon-sibility for the atrocity, going on a five-day fast of atonement. In doing so he earned the criticism (and in some cases the wrath) of many of his associates who believed the incident was a small blot on an otherwise peaceful movement. Moreover, many felt that the momentum was so much in favor of the freedom fighters that but for Gandhi's precipitate action, freedom would have been theirs by year end. Bhagat Singh himself was one such Gandhi admirer disillusioned by Gandhi's stance following the Chauri Chaura incident.

But Gandhi genuinely believed that a freedom won by bad means would be a bad freedom. He has been proved right by the travails of many a country that has freed itself from colonialism by adopting any means possible (Indonesia, Kenya, Algeria, to name but a few). The guns that were being used against the British by Indian freedom fighters who saw assassination of British officials as a reasonable response to British oppression, could tomorrow be turned against Indians. The need to build a polity where the discourse of ideas, not the discharge of weapons, would win the day was evident to Gandhi, though not always to many impatient but shortsighted hotheads across the country. Gandhi wrote:

> God has been abundantly kind to me. He had warned me that there is not yet in India that truthful and non-violent atmosphere which can justify mass disobedience which can be described as civil, which means gentle, truthful,

DOI: 10.1057/978-1-137-32516-7

humble, knowing, wilful yet loving, never criminal and hateful....God spoke clearly through Chauri Chaura.[8]

That the atrocity at Chauri Chaura happened despite Gandhi's efforts to keep the movement peaceful, that such misfirings were rare in a huge national movement involving hundreds of thousands, made no difference to Gandhi. He took total responsibility as the leader of the movement, and staked his entire career upon it:

> Let the opponent glory in our humiliation or so-called defeat. It is better to be charged with cowardice and weakness than to be guilty of denial of our oath and sin against God. It is a million times better to *appear* untrue before the world than to *be* untrue to ourselves.
>
> And so, for me the suspension of mass civil disobedience and other minor activities that were calculated to keep up excitement is not enough penance for my having been the instrument, however involuntary, of the brutal violence by the people at Chauri Chaura.[9]

Much as he may have believed in nonviolence, his action here, I feel, was just as much about orienting the freedom movement's sights in a highly visible manner, of setting the highest standards.[10] Frequently in our time, by contrast, the response to terrorist lawbreaking is a government hastening to dismantle any provisions of restraint on the statute book, often breaking laws itself, until over time the litany of misdeeds by authority appears to rival those of the terrorist.

# What would Gandhi do?

To get an idea of Gandhi's approach, we could go back and reread his works, *Hind Swaraj* in particular. For Gandhi alone grasped (and faced up to) the fundamental premise of terrorism—that it works only if the victims allow themselves to be terrorized, and therefore that the first, final, and decisive response to terror is the refusal to be afraid. "*That nation is great which rests its head upon death as its pillow*," he wrote in *Hind Swaraj*, (italics mine).[11] Confronted by fearlessness, the terrorist loses his biggest incentive, which is to instill fear in the population. The pluck and courage of the Londoners in the face of the Blitzkrieg did as much to blunt Hitler as any Allied offensive of World War II.

Lest someone should argue that Gandhi's methods are outworn in these postmodern days of smart phones, GPS, and assault rifles, we have already

DOI: 10.1057/978-1-137-32516-7

pointed out that Gandhi was quite conversant with not only the word "terrorism," which figures in several of his writings, but also its real manifestations. The reason is simple: his generation had seen terrorism first-hand. After all, the Bombay attacks of 2008 and the murders in Jallianwala Bagh of 1919 are similar: both unleashed lethal force suddenly and without provocation upon unarmed people. In the case of Jallianwala Bagh, General Dyer, who ordered the firing, answered in the affirmative when asked whether his purpose had been to "strike terror." The British repression of the 1930 Salt Satyagraha is one of the scenes shown truthfully and dramatically in the 1982 movie *Gandhi*. Discussion of "terrorism" in our time has somehow been confused by nonsense such as "state" and "nonstate actors." Gandhi was a lot more clearheaded. To him, a state could be as much a terrorist as an individual could, and he was unafraid to label it as such.

The second part of Gandhi's approach would be to seek justice. His statement that "My experience has shown me that we win justice quickest by rendering justice to the other party" contains a wealth of wisdom.[12] The heinousness of the attacks in Bombay or Bali, for instance, should not prevent soul searching about what happened in Gujarat, Kandhamal, and Kashmir (both government violence and anti-Hindu violence) or Kabul and Basra—and in India's case perhaps even stretching back to what happened in the Punjab and the Sikh pogroms after Indira Gandhi's death. A Gandhi would have spoken out against such pogroms, fasted, and perhaps even died in protest. Rammanohar Lohia called Gandhi the nation's sentinel. The absence of such a figure leads a people to fall prey to its own half-truths.

Finally, Gandhi would not care about whether someone else did right or wrong. For instance, the argument "But Pakistan/Al-Qaeda/LTTE does it" would carry no weight for him. He would insist that the nonterrorist state or individual not compound error (or terror) by adding its own to the tally.

The Mahatma would certainly oppose more repressive laws, censorship, detention without trial, arbitrary search and seizure, suspension of *habeas corpus*, and so on—all measures that governments in our age are ready to pursue at the slightest opportunity. Gandhi knew there could never be a bureaucratic solution to a political problem, just as no amount of armament could ever make up for an absence of heart. The best line in E. F. Schumacher's classic *Small Is Beautiful* is a quote attributed to Gandhi about the foolishness of trying to devise systems so perfect that no one would have to be good.

DOI: 10.1057/978-1-137-32516-7

In Gandhi's eyes, the ideal response of a state or a people to terrorism would be fearless determination, a "No pasarán" fortitude, coupled with a fierce commitment to the highest ideals in its own words and deeds. There is no surer antidote to terrorism in the long run; indeed, one might even say there is none other.

# Notes

1  Justin Raimondo, "When Satire Becomes Reality," September 9, 2009 (www. antiwar.com).

2  In her best-selling book, *The Shock Doctrine*, Naomi Klein describes in great detail the other aspect of the response to terror, the unquestioned shifting of wealth from public to private hands.

3  See Niranjan Ramakrishnan, "To Pindi Station," *Counterpunch*, Weekend Edition, January 4–6, 2008 (www.counterpunch.org/2008/01/04/to-pindi-station/).

4  A novel by R. K. Narayan, made into a movie by Dev Anand. The hero goes along with the pretense that he is a holy man, until circumstances demand his life on account of his masquerade.

5  The (longer) translation of the Gujarati version is in *Collected Works of Mahatma Gandhi*, Vol. 51, pp. 316–317.

6  *Young India*, March 31, 1931.

7  "What starts out here as a mass movement ends up as a racket, a cult, or a corporation." *The Temper of our Times*, Eric Hofer, Buccaneer Books, 1996.

8  *Collected Works of Mahatma Gandhi*, Vol. 26, p. 177.

9  *Collected Works of Mahatma Gandhi*, Vol. 26, p. 180 (emphasis in the original).

10 It also reveals Gandhi as a master of public relations. The contrast between the Raj's laggardly reaction to the mass murder by its senior officials at Jallianwala Bagh less than three years before and the alacrity with which its adversary responded to a stray incident of violence originating from its side could not have been laid out more clearly in front of the world.

11 *Hind Swaraj, Collected Works of Mahatma Gandhi*, Vol. 9, p. 295.

12 M. K. Gandhi, *The Story of My Experiments with Truth*, Chapter 17, "Passive Resistance."

DOI: 10.1057/978-1-137-32516-7

# 3
# Privatization...Privation... Privacy

Abstract: *The mantra of the post–Cold War era has been "privatize or perish," a slogan that has guided not only the three most populous countries in the world, China, India, and Russia, but even the so-called free enterprise democracies of old. Simultaneously, in many of the same regions, human deprivation and destitution seem to have gone hand in hand with galloping economic growth, while, on another front, human privacy has received short shrift. Many of Gandhi's warnings about the worship of economic well-being divorced from other considerations seem tailor-made for this perverse trifecta.*

Ramakrishnan, Niranjan. *Reading Gandhi in the Twenty-First Century*. New York: Palgrave Macmillan, 2013. DOI: 10.1057/9781137325150.

The syllogism runs something like this:

1 The foremost duty of the state is to foster economic growth, measured by an index called the growth rate.
2 The growth rate is maximized by granting unfettered freedom to the private sector to seek profits.
3 The role of government is therefore to dismantle any obstacles in the way of unbridled private gain.

As with many of their current notions, urban Indians have arrived at this sequence by looking abroad, in this case to America. Perhaps blinded a little in recent years by the strobe lights of the adulation that has made India the darling of Davos and similar venues, Indians appear not to have noticed a tableau that has been enacted simultaneously, and right before their eyes. Exactly such a puritanical pursuit of privatization, over the past three decades, has transformed the United States from the world's largest creditor to its largest debtor, laying waste to its fabled economy.

There is little doubt that the mantra of "growth above all else" has gripped the Indian intelligentsia. Whether from blinkered eye or cupidity of mind is but a detail. Strong too is the chokehold of this meme. So strong, indeed, that India's current prime minister thinks the rampant Maoist insurgency in the Indian heartland is the biggest problem facing the country because—get this—it could jeopardize the country's stellar growth rate of recent years.

The Indian prime minister is not alone. His American counterpart, who may owe his first term in no small part to the cratering of the US economy just before the election, is equally blasé. The 2008 American presidential candidates were evenly poised until the financial meltdown a couple of months before the polls. A direct consequence of the near-fundamentalist pursuit of privatization (deregulation) in the United States, the meltdown took the incumbent-party candidate's poll numbers down with it. Nevertheless, Barack Obama continues to speak the same language as every one of his predecessors since Reagan. His first address to the US Congress gave the mindset away. How could such a gifted speaker have so much difficulty saying that decent health was the birthright of every American? Instead, it was necessary because otherwise "we would break the budget." Or, "we should be educated so we may get a job in tomorrow's economy"—not so that we might be better citizens today.

DOI: 10.1057/978-1-137-32516-7

Just as Manmohan Singh's primary concern seemed not to be that people in his country were dying every day in an incipient civil war, Obama did not appear overly exercised about the impact a poor education would have on a society whose high level of civic literacy was once noted by de Tocqueville as the underpinning of its democratic polity. In both cases, the first clearly more egregious than the second, the head of government was telling us that his charter was economic advancement above all else.

As noteworthy is the fact that neither the Indian nor the American media made much of these respective statements, and that these statements did not appear to disturb the public in either country at all.

Neither the rulers, nor the intelligentsia, nor the people saw anything amiss in such an explicit redefinition of the government's purpose. To draw a parallel with Sherlock Holmes's dog that did not bark in the night, therein lay the news. The focus of the state had, tacitly, changed. No longer was it to protect the country's integrity or safeguard its people's rights—or even their lives. Instead it was to run interference on behalf of private interests to ensure they retained adequate means to make ample profits. In this scheme, education was nothing more than the provision of a suitably trained workforce—trained, that is, to be cogs in the global industrial empire, not educated to be proud and upstanding citizens of their country.

Welcome to a brave new world of politics and commerce, in which the ruling idea is that all good things (and good things alone) flow from the growth rate. In India, not only politicians but also academics, journalists, and businesspeople obsess over this point incessantly. But for economic growth, would the country have been able to showcase the 2010 Commonwealth Games, which proved that India was ready to rival China and its Olympic Games? Or gotten so near its current geostrategic preoccupation: permanent membership in the UN Security Council? It was a big deal to the prime minister that the head of each of the five current permanent members had visited India in the recent past.

Even at a 2010 news conference to reassure the nation in the wake of the 2G Scam, a mega-scandal concerning the licensing of frequencies to cell phone companies, the first words of the Indian prime minister were to reiterate his confidence that the high growth rate of the economy would be maintained.

It is sixty-five years since India became independent, and sixty years since the first of fifteen general elections to date. India is frequently

DOI: 10.1057/978-1-137-32516-7

hailed as the world's largest democracy, and rightly envied in quarters less fortunate for demonstrating that a developing country can support a viable and vibrant electoral polity. A novelty, this, then—that a poor nation, one that chose to burden itself with "overheads" such as due process, human rights legislation, a universal adult franchise, and a free press, could blossom economically too. As unlikely a tale is that of a land with so many languages and religions remaining united and thriving. In all the world, India alone can claim success on both counts. This, at least, is one viable narrative, and one hardly bereft of truth.

Then there is the other story. India leads the world in Swiss bank assets: Indian defaulters have reportedly salted away more than those of all other countries combined. Within the country, corruption is rampant at every level, with scams running into billions of dollars becoming quite commonplace. As author and journalist P. Sainath observes:

> The past 20 years[1] have seen unprecedented concentrations of wealth, often by awful means, mostly enabled by economic policy. The state stands reduced to a tool of corporate enrichment. It is there to facilitate private investment. Each budget is written for (and partly by) the corporate world. The last six budgets have gifted the corporates Rs.21 lakh crore[2] in concessions on just direct corporate income tax, customs and excise duties. In the same period, food subsidies and agriculture have suffered cuts.
>
> The neo-liberal economic framework assigns the state the role of wet nursing the corporate sector at public cost. This is why we live in the age of privatisation of just about everything. It is the state's mission to hand over scarce national resources of all kinds, land, water, spectrum, anything, to further bloat corporate profits. It is this process of peddling a nation's resources to private agents on preferential terms that is the main source of corruption in our time. The scams are the symptoms; a state that serves corporations, not citizens, is the disease.[3]

The prospect of quick (and hitherto unknown amounts of) lucre has left no section of the Indian elite untouched.

In India and in America, a common narrative has gained ground: that government is the enemy, that it can do no right, that the private sector is efficient, that the way to progress is for government to step aside and allow the private sector complete and total control over the nation's destiny. Doing so makes for better living and "freedom."

To what degree is this true? Perhaps it would not be unwise to look at the results from a laboratory where precisely this experiment has been carried out for the past thirty years: the United States of America.

DOI: 10.1057/978-1-137-32516-7

To begin with only the most egregious aspect of profiteering, the past ten years have been years of war without victory, but a decade in which the nature of the US military has undergone an enormous change. War has been privatized to a degree previously unimagined. Many of the functions that would be presumed to belong to the traditional armed forces have been outsourced to private companies. Names such as Blackwater and CACI have been much in the news for their shenanigans. In essence, war has provided the perfect cover to convey astronomical amounts of public wealth into the hands of private contractors.

Yet the transfer of wealth, the charges of fraud and abuse, are only one aspect of the privatization of war. More troublesome is the political angle. Many of these private contractors have been given a virtual carte blanche with regard to their actions, accompanied by a freedom from liability and accountability that might be the envy of a Pontius Pilate.

Meanwhile in the United States, a thirty-year onslaught has made a joke of the notion that corporations ought to pay taxes commensurate with all the benefits they receive from the state. The result is budget deficits at every level of government. This situation is now being "rectified" by cutting down on wages, benefits, health care, and retirement commitments to ordinary working people. There is no money for infrastructure maintenance; some cities are even decommissioning essentials such as firefighting and policing. Many other vital services are being scaled back in the interest of "balancing the budget," affecting schools, public health facilities, and libraries.

The political import of privatization is thus clear. Judging by what the "privatize or perish" ideology has wrought in the United States, there is little to recommend it even as a vehicle for economic renaissance. To paraphrase Gandhi in *Hind Swaraj*, *privatization seeks to increase economic well-being and it fails miserably even in doing so.*

With all its claims as a jealous deity that brooks no rival, it would be one thing if economic growth brought about enormous and permanent good. This is, however, far from the case. Whether in the United States, Russia, or India, the gap between the rich and the poor has only grown wider with privatization. In a near–Freudian slip of etymology, "privation" appears to be a concomitant of blind privatization.

This needs to be explained a little, because the promoters of privatization would point to the huge numbers of people that privatized corporate economic activity has ostensibly moved from poverty to a better life in places such as China and India. On the face of it, there is certainly

DOI: 10.1057/978-1-137-32516-7

evidence of people buying far more consumer goods in these countries. At the same time, there is a monstrous trend of farmer suicides in India, and of prostitution and corruption being the fastest-growing areas of the Chinese economy. This is quite apart from the larger question of what is being sacrificed in the quest for growth.

Liberalization of the economy is a code word for the state withdrawing from supervising the activity of the private sector, which includes taking up for those affected by its furious and single-minded drive for maximum profit. The tally of those injured along the path includes not only farmers, workers, and students but also those even less capable of protest—the environment, animals, birds, and so on.

Thus it is that in India, prime farmland is granted to set up SEZs (special economic zones), groundwater and river pollution by effluents is winked at in the name of protecting industries, and genetically modified grain is pushed. The people, animals, birds, and fish ruined or killed in this macho march to superpowerhood count for nothing. Educated Indians are not shy to say—the less lettered ones on Internet forums and their more erudite cousins in the more refined print outlets—that this is the price of progress. Many seem genuinely convinced that a great favor is being done to the tribals or other villagers whose lives are disrupted or even lost in this upheaval.

On the other side of the Himalayas, the scale of China's coming environmental holocaust has been the subject of many an essay. Its consequences will be with us for several lifetimes.

As in "The Man That Corrupted Hadleyburg," a short story by Mark Twain, the lore and lure of untold wealth has made short work of all the old ethics of simplicity and self-restraint in the two most ancient civilizations on the planet.[4] Post-privatization, both India and China have experienced a burst of graft and crony capitalism beyond anything seen in earlier times. The fire sale of Russia's state resources during the Boris Yeltsin years is part of the historical record. In America, the abnegation of the state was carried out in characteristically state-of-the-art fashion: it first removed all the regulations that prevented private entities from mulcting the citizen through the most extreme kinds of speculation, and then, when this resulted in widespread financial mayhem, proceeded to use public funds (read: the public's funds) to bail out the perpetrators of these very scams.[5] Indeed, the world's oldest democracy has even gone on to privatize large segments of its electoral process, an artifact that is still cited by some political observers as putting the results of a couple of recent presidential elections into question.

DOI: 10.1057/978-1-137-32516-7

The Indian commentator Jawed Naqvi has noted that as far as India is concerned, many of the cases where corruption was tackled and its practitioners brought to book occurred during the so-called pre-liberalization era; few instances of such visible punishment have taken place in the privatized economy, even though the amounts involved are orders of magnitude larger.[6] The stain of financial scandal now runs the entire facade of the Indian ruling class: politicians, industrialists, the military, and even the judiciary. Scams abound up and down the country's social and political structure, and a muckraker could take his pick all the way from the municipal corporation to the highest corridors of power in Delhi, with the amounts involved ballooning at each ascent.

Current wisdom dates the start of India's growth explosion to the time it began "opening up" its economy to the world, starting in the early 1990s. Instead of the government (in the name of the public) controlling its commanding heights, more and more of the economy was turned over to the private sector. Simultaneously, longstanding suspicion of foreign interests, natural to a poster child for colonial exploitation, was quickly replaced by an avid and almost reverential wooing of foreign capital.

In what seems like a contest to prove their devotion to the deity of the economic growth rate, parties of ostensibly opposite stripes all strike the same chord when they come to power. Even when one party has been voted out and replaced with the opposition, there has been no letup in the march of privatization. Practically the first words of any incoming administration are a reiteration of its dedication to "economic reforms," a euphemism for further privatization. Under a variety of state and central governments spanning virtually the entire spectrum of political parties, the Indian state has marched in lock step to acquiesce in tax holidays and limitation of labor rights, at times even allowing private communities with their own bylaws and police forces and economic empowerment zones in which some provisions of the Indian Constitution may be held in partial abeyance.

We can see, then, even in the relatively short span of thirty years during which this new religion of unfettered privatization has gained ascendance in the United States—and during the past twenty years in other major countries such as Russia, China, and India—that its legacies are highly uneven in the short term, and highly detrimental in the long term, with resulting disparities that may well rend society itself.

Gandhi saw and rejected this red herring of a consumer utopia of endless wants and untold compromises a hundred years ago. To Gandhi

DOI: 10.1057/978-1-137-32516-7

this was obvious because the whole matter came back to his central theme, the freedom of the individual. He saw in the pursuit of wealth to the exclusion of other concerns a debasing of the human soul. In *Hind Swaraj*, he wrote, "Hinduism, Islam, Zoroastrianism, Christianity and all other religions teach that we should remain passive about worldly pursuits and active about godly pursuits, that we should set a limit to our worldly ambitions and that our religious ambition should be illimitable. Our activity should be directed into the latter channel." Indeed, Gandhi's concerns regarding the mindset of growth rate economics and the industrial/consumer society that sprang from it (and that it sprang from) began in his youth. According to his autobiography, the following words of the *Bhagavad Gita* made a deep impression on him when he was first introduced to it as a student in London:

[The pursuit of sense objects]

Lets noble purpose go, and saps the mind,

Till purpose, mind, and man are all undone.

A prosaic interpretation would note that the warning to remain "passive about worldly pursuits," or about the consequences of hankering after sense objects, stands foursquare athwart the path to high economic growth rates. Gandhi's suspicion of schemes that would bring huge economic welfare sprang from this simple and profound understanding: for all its attraction, even beneficence, on the way in, this is what lay at the end of the path—the undoing of the individual. It was perhaps why Gandhi remained chary of anything that promised material well-being in exchange for human freedom. Thus in his response to Henry Ford 's idea of "decentralization of industry by the use of electric power, with hundreds and thousands of small, neat, smokeless villages, dotted with factories, run by village communities," when asked why he would have any objection, Gandhi replied with what boiled down to a simple question: "Who would control the switch?" He added that to the extent that large industry was necessary, it should be under public control.

A 2011 article in the *Guardian* referred to another writer with a horror of "bigness." Born in the year *Hind Swaraj* was written, Leopold Kohr (1909–1994) had pointed out the incompatibility of human freedom with large systems, economic, political, or social. In the words of Paul Kingsnorth:

We have now reached the point that Kohr warned about over half a century ago: the point where "instead of growth serving life, life must now serve

DOI: 10.1057/978-1-137-32516-7

growth, perverting the very purpose of existence." Kohr's "crisis of bigness" is upon us and, true to form, we are scrabbling to tackle it with more of the same: closer fiscal unions, tighter global governance, geoengineering schemes, more economic growth. Big, it seems, is as beautiful as ever to those who have the unenviable task of keeping the growth machine going.[7]

In the rush to front-loaded benefits in the age of privatization, Gandhi's question "Who would control the switch?" is, unfortunately, seldom asked. In the quest for economic growth and creature comforts many things are sacrificed, including hard-won freedoms and human privileges.

Chief among these is the right to privacy. Few people have captured the tragedies of our age better than the late Joe Bageant, the author of *Deer Hunting with Jesus—Dispatches from America's Class War.*[8] In an essay called "Algorithms and Red Wine—Is the 'Digital Hive' a Soft Totalitarian State?" Bageant asks a question that should trouble us all greatly, although, worryingly, it doesn't seem to at all. It would have certainly troubled Gandhi.

> Meanwhile, we have our social networking software to better weave us into the hive. Social networking software, now there's a term that should scare the piss out of anyone with an IQ over 40. It means the database as hive reality. Facebook, online banking, shopping, porn, years of one's life play-ing electronic games or whatever, online dating and reducing romance and companionship to fit the software. Or 4,000 Facebook "friends," data on 4,000 Americans voluntarily collected for Facebook corporation. The con-cept of "friends" is cheapened, rendered meaningless as it passes through a database. In fact, all human experience is cheapened by that process.

As Bageant says, this is private information on an individual, collected, stored, sold, and deployed by private firms for their own profit. The combi-nation of privatization and technology has stripped an individual of all pri-vacy. Every action of the denizen of a modern consumer state is trackable, and usable without any requirement of legal authority. With the arrival of modern algorithms for face recognition, every moment of an individual, too, is in some private hands, easily replicable and transferable as needed.

In 1978, an Indian student friend of mine went to visit China. An unusually enterprising fellow, he had learned some Chinese before he went, since he wanted to mingle with average Chinese citizens and get a feel for the "real" country, instead of just taking in the sights like the usual tourist. Entering the country at Canton (Guangzhou), he soon

DOI: 10.1057/978-1-137-32516-7

managed to give the authorities the slip and disappear into the city. He regaled us with stories of how he caught the train to Beijing, a long journey during which he interacted with the local crowd, and how he was surprised to hear the Raj Kapoor hit song "Awara Hoon" piped through the train's speakers. The point is, such anonymity can no longer be hoped for today.[9]

Of all its perils, it seems to me, the elimination of privacy and the availability of every individual action for commercial ends are two of the most pernicious and longstanding of the privatization ideology's impacts. The consequent transformation of the individual from citizen to commercial cog (as either consumer or provider) and its effect on the nature of life in the modern liberal democratic state are among the surest hallmarks of the age.

# Notes

1   Since the advent of neoliberal economic policies in India.

2   Rupees 21 trillion, approximately $420 billion.

3   P. Sainath, "The Gang That Couldn't Shoot Straight," *The Hindu*, July 8, 2011.

4   "Needless to say, the current concern over corruption is partly a by-product of the current triumph of democratic capitalism, with its unparalleled economic expansion and wealth creation. Our age has been called 'La Troisième Belle Epoch,' in which the expectation is that the world will be both free and rich—and the poor will become rich and the rich richer, by virtue of our laissez-faire economic system" (from the foreword by J. McDonald Williams to Mark Twain, "The Man That Corrupted Hadleyburg," 1999; https://www.ttf.org/index.php?page=shop.product_details&product_id=76&flypage=flypage_new.tpl&pop=0&option=com_virtuemart&Itemid=54&redirected=1&Itemid=54).

5   See Matt Taibbi, *Griftopia: A Story of Bankers, Politicians, and the Most Audacious Power Grab in American History*, Spiegel & Grau, 2010.

6   Jawed Naqvi, "India's Free-Market Mantra" (http://dawn.com/2010/09/20/indias-free-market-mantra/).

7   Paul Kingsnorth, "This Economic Collapse Is a 'Crisis of Bigness,'" *Guardian*, September 26, 2011.

8   Joe Bageant, *Deer Hunting with Jesus—Dispatches from America's Class War*, Crown, 2007.

9   It is said that Chairman Mao declared *Awara*, the film this song is from, to be his favorite movie.

DOI: 10.1057/978-1-137-32516-7

# 4
# Globalization...of What?

Abstract: *What's not to like about globalization? Nothing, if you think it is simply the ability to get anything from anywhere. Much, if the scope of the damage you can now do is worldwide. Gandhi foresaw both the economic and the moral hazards of globalization; his vision of globalization even figures in his choice of poetry.*

Ramakrishnan, Niranjan. *Reading Gandhi in the Twenty-First Century*. New York: Palgrave Macmillan, 2013. DOI: 10.1057/9781137325150.

What's not to like about the age of globalization? Sitting in Mombasa or Mumbai these days, you can order in Szechuan for lunch, dine out at a cantina in the evening, stock your cellar with wines from Chile or California, and place orders on the Hong Kong, Chicago, or London stock exchange using your "Made in Malaysia" or "Made in Taiwan" cell phone.

Anyone suggesting twenty years ago that such things would shortly come about would have been laughed off the stage. Would anyone have imagined that from your living room in Omaha you could find an inexpensive tutor from some small town in India to help with your child's algebra homework, or that a young man in a bachelor pad in Silicon Valley could fix himself up with a Russian bride? Now it all starts to look like the promise in Kipling's line "Yours is the Earth and everything that's in it."

What could be so terrible about all this?

Nothing much, if you also think there is not much wrong with millions of tourists running their excursion buses and SUVs up and down previously pristine Himalayan hillsides, with petrol fumes and plastic wrappers banishing forever the undisturbed tranquility of ages. It's their Earth too, after all, and isn't that a nice feeling to have.

From Gandhi's viewpoint, it all boils down to the question "Of what do you claim ownership?" Is it the temporary (as we shall see) affordability of the exotic or the permanent devastation of unseen peoples and lands? It's all very easy to feel as if the world is your oyster when you travel to faraway places, staying in resorts possibly built on some environmentally sensitive spot.

Many arguments can be made against globalization, but one of the strongest in my view is the universal willingness—and growing capacity—to trash unseen corners of the world. A columnist from Pakistan laments the vanished ancient and sacred natural pool at Kataasraj in the Salt Range.[1] It is now bone dry because three cement plants set up in this pristine region to meet the growing demand for cement in Afghanistan have used up all the water. Some years back Ingmar Lee wrote an eyewitness account of the pollution of the Himalayas as a result of tourism, development, and military deployment.[2] Describing his trip to Badrinath, a Hindu shrine in the mountain ranges, Ananda Vardhana, a lifelong hiker and mountaineer, writes of the desecration by plastic that neither the piety of religion nor the majesty of nature seemed to have the power to forfend:

> Mana is the last border town. This is where Pandavas ended their journey on the earth before ascending into heaven. Bheem Kund is a roaring water fall

DOI: 10.1057/978-1-137-32516-7

where the falling water has created a wondrous deep well....Bheema, with his superb strength, is said to have created the well with a mighty blow of his mace. I was surprised to see empty Frito Lay chip packets strewn among the rocks below. I then realized that the Pandavas, just before Swargarohana[3], were told to leave all their earthly belongings, Lay's chips being one of them, since "no one can eat just one" there was plenty of it. Tourists in India are superb rock climbers. Even on the vertical surface of the precipice where a fall would mean certain death, one could see true artistic feats. There they had declared their true love and devotion. The question might not have been, "Can you get me the moon?", but, "Can you paint my name using indelible paint for centuries to come?" Yes, graffiti marred the border with the strewn colorful plastic all around.[4]

In other, equally precious parts of the world, the trashing is institutionalized, far more systemic and systematic than a stray vandal immortalizing a once-in-a-lifetime jaunt. Rare ecosystems are leveled in the glorious cause of keeping the shelves stacked with fatty snacks for some already overfed teenager. A supply chain stretching halfway round the planet demands some fifty square miles of rainforest be turned into farmland each day[5] to grow the feed for factory-farmed cattle that become hamburgers. Since they happen far away, neither the devastation of the Amazon wilderness nor the wanton cruelty to the animal is felt by the supposed monarch of our times, the universal consumer. The worst thing about globalization is that it allows one to do harm from far away, often without even realizing it.

Protectionism, the supposed antithesis of globalization, has come in for spirited indictment by the press in previously protected economies. Writers point to a bygone era of long lines and domestic inefficiencies, of back-alley hustlers peddling foreign-made goods, and of a few in high positions enjoying the pleasures of imported wares to the envious looks of shut-out gawkers. "Thank goodness," they sigh, "finally we have seen the light and realized that we could not have remained in that demented regime of nationalism forever." "Besides," they exult, "look at what we have accomplished! How much we export! How we have spread our name for industries that just a few years ago we did not even know existed!"

The traditional promoters of the fight against trade hurdles have been the nations of the West. With the collapse of the Soviet Union in the early 1990s came the realization by the two most populous countries of the world that they would have to do business—quite literally—with the

DOI: 10.1057/978-1-137-32516-7

United States in this changed world. The new equation altered the old state of affairs in a mere twenty years. For instance, the United States, which until a few decades ago made 80 percent of the goods and services it used, now imports practically everything it consumes. Services too. For a while there was some brave talk of the loss of manufacturing being merely a recognition of the United States and Europe as the intellectual powerhouse shedding the more humdrum elements of business to lesser nations. This facade is sustainable no longer, with the massive exodus of white-collar jobs from the West to back offices in other countries showing up in lost tax revenues, and in ensuing news stories of American city halls going bankrupt.

One industry magnate who saw disaster coming was Andrew Grove, former CEO of Intel Corporation, interviewed in 2005 by the *New York Times*:

> Then he moved to the subject of his latest obsession: globalization. Will it surprise you to know that this refugee from Hungary, whose company derives 70 percent of its revenue from places other than the United States, is a bear on the potential consequences of globalization on this country? He is.
>
> "I don't think there is a good outcome," he said. "I looked up a quote for you. 'If you don't believe that [globalization] changes the average wages in America, you believe in the tooth fairy.' Do you know who said that? Paul Samuelson, age 90."
>
> Although mainstream economic thought holds that America's history of creativity and entrepreneurialism will allow it to adapt to the rise of such emerging economies as India and China, Mr. Grove thinks that is so much wishful thinking. In his view, globalization will not only finish off what's left of American manufacturing, but will turn so-called knowledge workers, which was supposed to be America's competitive advantage, into just another global commodity.[6]

"So what?" one might ask, echoing the start of British columnist George Monbiot's oft-quoted piece "The Flight to India": "If you live in a rich nation in the English-speaking world, and most of your work involves a computer or a telephone, don't expect to have a job in five years' time."[7] No great tragedy, this, Monbiot went on; this was just repayment time: "Throughout the 18th and 19th centuries, India was forced to supply raw materials to Britain's manufacturers, but forbidden to produce competing finished products.... We are rich because the Indians are poor.... Now the jobs we stole 300 years ago are returning to India."

DOI: 10.1057/978-1-137-32516-7

Monbiot's article shows the unwitting convergence of the free market enthusiast (which is to say, the Establishment in every country) and the postmodern left-winger on the matter of globalism. One believes that in free trade lies the salvation of lagging lands, while the other sees the stripping of jobs in the West as a kind of reparation. As William Lind and William Piper put it in a recent essay, "Economically, the Establishment stands for globalism, which averages the once prosperous economies of the West with those of the rest of the world. They come up, but we go down."[8]

The word "average" is significant here; it is such faith in gross measurement that is the touchstone of so many well-intentioned proponents of globalization. Going from averages to specifics, there is the ongoing struggle in Orissa, India, where a Korean Corporation called POSCO is seeking to take over lands currently cultivated for betel leaves for a $12 billion steel plant. The Indian government and others supporting the project doubtless see it as a shining example of globalization raising the gross domestic product of the nation, which is one of the key measures of how things are going.

A globalist viewpoint on this matter is presented in a brief first-hand account of the anti-POSCO movement. The writer, Sampad Mahapatra, begins by asking:

> Can a small minority of 4000-odd people hold the state and the country to ransom? Do they have any right to stand in the way of the biggest Foreign Direct Investment in India, the Rs 52,000 crore South Korean project that would generate huge amounts of revenue and employment and benefit millions of people?...And in the process, embarrassing a government which is only trying to take control over the land it owns and for the larger public good.

He answers his own rhetorical question with a macabre example from the same region:

> Kondh tribals in Orissa used to sacrifice one member of their community each year to ensure a bumper "turmeric" crop. The gory ritual that involved beheading of the person and sprinkling of his blood on the nascent turmeric crop was called the "Meria"!

Mahapatra concludes by asking:

> Would we be any less barbaric today if we believe the government is authorized to trample on people and their basic right to livelihood and dignity just because they refuse to fall in line or hail the $12 billion steel project, the

DOI: 10.1057/978-1-137-32516-7

biggest FDI in India as a manna from the Heaven that will "change the face of Orissa" and wipe out hunger, poverty and backwardness with its magical steel wand. If 4 crore people stand to benefit why can't 4000 people be gracious enough to give in? If they don't they can to go to hell.[9]

Gandhi believed in globalization. Looked at one way, this was one of the strongest criticisms leveled against him. He thought that human beings everywhere were the same in that they had a heart and a conscience. His precept of *Antyodaya*, or concern for the welfare of the "last man," was rooted in this idea.

Equally strongly was he opposed to the idea of globalization as an economic mantra. His opposition was a natural outgrowth of his paramount preoccupation: the liberty of the individual. When an individual's livelihood or even life depended on what was happening thousands of miles away, clearly that individual had, to that extent, forfeited freedom of action. Gandhi's globalism shines through even brighter when he makes clear that this is no parochial or nationalistic instinct; he is willing to say that even within the same country, he would prefer everything an individual consumed to be locally obtained, perhaps within a five-mile radius. In one place Gandhi writes that if one is dissatisfied with the services of one's barber, rather than go to some faraway city to get a good haircut, one should bring someone from there to one's own neighborhood and get the local barber trained. The "Vow of *Swadeshi*" says exactly this:

> I suggest to you we are departing from one of the sacred laws of our being when we leave our neighbour and go out somewhere else in order to satisfy our wants. If a man comes from Bombay here and offers you wares, you are not justified in supporting the Bombay merchant or trader so long as you have got a merchant at your very door, born and bred in Madras. That is my view of swadeshi. In your village, so long as you have got your village-barber, you are bound to support him to the exclusion of the finished barber who may come to you from Madras. If you find it necessary that your village-barber should reach the attainment of the barber from Madras, you may train him to that. Send him to Madras by all means, if you wish, in order that he may learn his calling. Until you do that, you are not justified in going to another barber. That is swadeshi.

"All well and good," you say, "but what about things that cannot be obtained locally? Say, petroleum—or uranium?" Gandhi anticipates this question in the very next sentence:

> So, when we find that there are many things that we cannot get in India, we must try to do without them. We may have to do without many things

DOI: 10.1057/978-1-137-32516-7

which we may consider necessary, but believe me, when you have that frame of mind, you will find a great burden taken off your shoulders, even as the Pilgrim did in that inimitable book, *Pilgrim's Progress*: There came a time when the mighty burden that the Pilgrim was carrying on his shoulders unconsciously dropped from him, and he felt a freer man than he was when he started on the journey. So will you feel freer men than you are now, immediately you adopt this swadeshi life.[10]

It is interesting to note how Gandhi rejects globalization on the basis of *Swadeshi*. The word *Swadeshi* is traditionally associated with choosing to buy Indian products over foreign. But Gandhi's interpretation, as evident from the quotation above, is deeper and wider. *Swadeshi* here is not restricted to anything Indian. It is entirely of a piece with his view that the individual's freedom (Gandhi might have called it "liberation" or *moksha*) is always the ultimate goal. This is but one example of his instinct for genuine globalism that he demonstrated many times over. He had no desire for India to colonize other lands as Britain had colonized India. He did not see an India that exploited other countries as any part of his economic outlook.

Gandhi's globalism would shake its head at the irony of an avowed globalist such as Barack Obama calling down drone strikes on far-off places. Gandhi might see this as a rather curious way of being a globalist: take whatever you want from wherever, and feel free to punish anybody anywhere who opposes you. Which might be, when you think about it, the Bush doctrine in a nutshell.

Gandhi would not be fooled for one instant by the clamor about the planet being bound together by globalization. Shunning the rose-tinted glasses, he might note that globalization has created a new nation. It is the first truly diverse, multicultural, multinational, multiethnic nation in the world. Call it Elitia. Its citizens have transcended the bonds of birth, nation, culture, ethnicity, and so on, swearing allegiance to none but the One True God of Universal Consumption, heads bowed daily at the Diocese of Technology, a wholly owned subsidiary of the Church of Globalization. Gandhi was too alive to the mischief of every single one of these sirens to be taken in by shibboleths.

As well versed in the Bible as in the *Gita*, the Mahatma might have suggested that a truer test of globalization lay in a Solomonic proposition: the real globalism lay in sacrificing oneself for anyone in distress anywhere, not in the notion that the world was one's oyster for economic exploitation and reward. "There is no limit to extending our service to

DOI: 10.1057/978-1-137-32516-7

our neighbours across our State-made frontiers. God never made those frontiers."[11] He might have noted too that many impulses that are noble when they arise in individual hearts become sullied when mummified into permanent institutions for assured gain. Thus the difference between the freedom brigades in the Spanish Civil War, Lafayette fighting by Washington's side, or Pearson and Andrews coming over to help Gandhi, on the one hand, and World Bank consultants and WTO administrators paving the way for the unfettered flow of goods and capital, on the other.

For Gandhi, the simple question would be: "What are you in it for? Are you in it to sacrifice, or to profit?" This is an idea expressed in Gandhi's favorite hymn, *Vaishnava Jana To Tene Hi Kahiye, Peerha parayi jane je*: "Call them alone people of God who know the woes of others as their own." And when we ask ourselves what the motive is for globalization in our time, the question resolves itself on its own.

# Notes

1  Ayaz Amir, "What the Ages Couldn't Accomplish…," *The News International*, May 4, 2012.
2  http://www.counterpunch.org/2006/08/23/india-s-occupation-of-ladakh/.
3  Literally, "ascent to heaven."
4  Ananda Vardhana, "Hemkund—Ascent to Eternity," July 2007 (http://www. indogram.com/?centerpiece=__mag/oped/191.html&city=smf).
5  "Rainforest Facts" (http://www.rain-tree.com/facts.htm).
6  Andrew Grove in an interview with Joseph Nocera, "From Intel to Health Care and Beyond," *New York Times*, July 30, 2005.
7  George Monbiot, "The Flight to India," 2003 (http://www.monbiot. com/2003/10/21/the-flight-to-india/).
8  William S. Lind and William S. Piper, "Alternate History," *The American Conservative* June 14, 2011. (http://www.amconmag.com/blog/alternate-history/).
9  Sampad Mahapatra, "Orissa's Corporate 'Meria,'" (http://social.ndtv.com/ SampadMahapatra/permalink/49821).
10  The "Vow of *Swadeshi*" from a speech on "Ashram Vows" at the YMCA, Madras, on February 16, 1916. Reproduced in *Collected Works of Mahatma Gandhi*, Vol. 15, pp. 171–172.
11  Speech at a meeting in Lausanne, December 8, 1931. Reproduced in *Collected Works of Mahatma Gandhi*, Vol. 54, p. 267.

DOI: 10.1057/978-1-137-32516-7

# 5

# A Fundamental(ist) Irony

Abstract: *The Taliban's destruction of the Buddhas of Bamiyan caused worldwide outrage, but there are many different kinds of fundamentalism, some far more powerful, and far more destructive, than the atavistic enthusiasms of a bunch of tribal zealots.*

▶

Ramakrishnan, Niranjan. *Reading Gandhi in the Twenty-First Century*. New York: Palgrave Macmillan, 2013. DOI: 10.1057/9781137325150.

No one with the faintest historical or cultural pulse could have remained unshaken by the Taliban's move to destroy all statues in Afghanistan, including two famous ones of the Buddha dating back some 1,500 years. As savagery unfolded before its cable-glazed eyes, the world watched, distressed but helpless. Calloused as our collective psyche has become, we are still capable of mustering some outrage when we see a piece of cultural history deliberately destroyed in the name of religion.

India's anguish, too, and indeed that of the civilized world, was expressed in a forthright statement by its External Affairs Ministry (never mind that three government ministers were neck-deep in the razing of a centuries-old monument, with several of their colleagues and supporters calling for encores elsewhere—but then hypocrisy, not irony, is our defining national trait).

Even as the Taliban issued its orders to blast cultural treasures in Afghanistan, the Union Budget was being presented in India, and had he descended Bhageerath-like with the Ganga itself,[1] finance minister Yashwant Sinha could not have been hailed more as a savior. On the same pages they toasted the budget, the papers bewailed the imminent demise of the Bamiyan Buddhas. Mr. Sinha, in the meantime, had won everyone's hearts with the promise of unfettered "development," a euphemism for unbridled consumption. The nation rejoiced in the fact that there would be more and cheaper cars on the road. And more buildings, more industries, more luxury—the millennium was getting here at last.

Reluctantly, almost bashfully, but with a gentle insistence, irony was heading front-stage that day. As we mourned an ancient statue or two, we were celebrating decisions that would accelerate the destruction of an ozone layer eons older. But irony should have become accustomed to such inexorable prominence of late. As we decry forced religious conversions, we have no difficulty demanding that people leave their ancient lands to accommodate our dams. Even as we proclaim our heritage from the rooftops, we pull down century-old trees, pockmark our virgin hillsides with buildings, and pollute our rivers. In our defense, though, we can claim that in this race to the bottom, India is only an eager and willing convert, Gandhi's dreams notwithstanding, and by no means alone. No country is exempt; if any nation does not want to be part of this master plan, its leadership is calumnied and blackballed, and every effort is made to break its will and force it to pay homage to this One God.

DOI: 10.1057/978-1-137-32516-7

The Taliban are an unsophisticated, easily identified, source of intolerance. No one can defend their aims, or their means. They may have destroyed some irreplaceable statues, but at least their poison is obvious and its scope limited. On the other hand, our newest, fastest-growing—and, yes, totalitarian—religion is insidious; its appeal and reach universal. It has many names—globalization, development, progress—but whatever the name, its basis remains the same: greed and consumerism. And it is wont to destroy our heritage as surely as the Taliban.

If you put a frog into a pot of boiling water, it will try to jump out immediately, but if you put the frog into the same pot with the water at room temperature, and then raise the heat slowly and steadily, it will die without attempting to escape. Gandhi, who worried a lot about the correct means, was no fool with regard to the correct ends: "He is no follower of ahimsa...who does not care a straw if he kills a man by inches by deceiving him in a trade, or who...in order to do a supposed good to his country does not mind killing off a few officials."[2]

The Taliban leaders may be criminally deranged fanatics for destroying the Bamiyan Buddhas. But are American leaders visionaries exactly when they call for oil wells in the Arctic National Refuge, because they have no notion that their energy problem lies with their country's endless appetites? When a single nation that already accounts for 25 percent of the world's energy consumption complains of energy shortages and looks ravenously for more (blithely talking about "our oil" when alluding to the Persian Gulf), one need seek no further evidence that we live in a crazy world.

As for India, it is pathetic to see the absence of any serious public debate on the nature, logic, and consequences of development. In the early years of independence, the word stood for providing our people with the essentials for living. Now, regardless of political stripe, public figures in the land of Gandhi (who visualized India as a *Karma Bhumi* (land of duty), not a *Bhoga Bhumi* (land of luxury)) appear united in their wish to see their country somehow become affluent, high-rolling, high-flying, living high off the hog. Development, not religion, is the opiate of our times. No price is too high to spread this creed of consumption, and anything standing in its way is to be eradicated with missionary zeal. Sometimes the price is searing, as on the day India welcomed George W. Bush. Was this the same country whose prime minister had once addressed a joint session of the US Congress with the following words: "Where freedom is menaced or justice threatened or where aggression takes place, we cannot be and shall not be neutral"?[3]

DOI: 10.1057/978-1-137-32516-7

Let us put Nehru's words (1949) in context: here is the leader of a country still dependent on foreign aid for food, militarily negligible, a country of crushing poverty, invited to address the Congress of the United States. We watch him treat the superpower as an equal, recalling it to its highest values. It lionizes him. JFK's first State of the Union address (1961) invokes the "soaring idealism of Nehru." In 1962, C. Rajagopalachari (also known as Rajaji, an associate of the Mahatma and a political opponent of Nehru) visits the United States and the Soviet Union to promote the importance of nuclear disarmament. President Kennedy listens with rapt attention, later recalling his meeting with Rajagopalachari as "one of the most civilizing influences on me."[4]

This was an era when India was regarded everywhere as a moral superpower, even if it was poor in material wealth. The authority India wielded on the world stage was lopsided, totally out of proportion to its military or economic power. Why was this so? Every country wants its people to eat well, but India, like America, represented something more: the inspiration of high purpose. Gandhi's freedom movement set minds everywhere on fire. This was followed, after independence, by Nehru's forging of the entirely new paradigm of nonalignment, whereby India refused to trade political allegiance for economic blandishment.

Paradoxically, today, when India is an expanding power, exporting not just food but steel, with rising incomes, foreign acquisitions, and a nuclear bomb, it is often viewed as nothing more than "a country with a middle class of 400 million." And the moral voice? It hasn't been heard from in years. There was courage in rags, but there is only meekness and timidity in riches. And the bomb, far from emboldening, seems only to have induced servility. Thus, to regularize a nuclear deal with the United States, among other economic aims, India rolled out the red carpet to an American president who had, to many, sullied everything inspiring about America.

When Bush invaded Iraq in 2003, India remained mute, likely considering the forfeiture of any potential contracts in postwar Iraq. How electrifying it would have been for India to resume its role as the world's moral superpower, to condemn the invasion from the rooftops, to recall its ambassador from Washington. India could once more have become the beacon of the world.

But that is unimaginable today. For today's India is rich, nuclear—and fearful. In the words of my father, K. G. Ramakrishnan, "Where there was the torment of the soul, there now was the swagger of the body."

DOI: 10.1057/978-1-137-32516-7

Where once the country of 400 million "subjects" overthrew the mightiest empire known to history, the weight of 400 million "consumers" forces a free nation to acquiesce in a fresh imperialism. Rammanohar Lohia noted long ago that the struggle of the twentieth century was between non-cooperation and the atom bomb. Were he alive today, he might have cast it somewhat differently, as a battle between moral self-respect and modern consumption. Far from not remaining neutral in the face of aggression, as Nehru said, we see an India actually feting the aggressor.

As Gandhi wrote, "How heavy is the toll of sins and wrongs that wealth, power and prestige exact from man."

# Notes

1  As Prometheus stole fire from the gods, Bhageerath in Indian mythology brought the river Ganges down from the heavens.

2  *On Ahimsa: Reply to Lala Lajpat Rai*, October 1916. *Collected Works of Mahatma Gandhi*, Vol. 15, p. 253.

3  Jawaharlal Nehru, addressing a joint session of US House and Senate, October 13, 1949.

4  Rajaji – A Life by Rajmohan Gandhi. Also, Pasricha, Ashu (2008) *Encyclopaedia Eminent Thinkers* (vol. 15: The Political Thought Of C. Rajagopalachari). Concept Publishing Company. ISBN 818069495X, ISBN 978–81–8069–495–0, p. 71.

DOI: 10.1057/978-1-137-32516-7

# 6
# Environmentalism

Abstract: *In an era when all those in power keep emphasizing their commitment to environmentalism, the environment seems to be declining faster than one can say "climate change". Gandhi was also an early environmentalist, but from a spiritual viewpoint, not a scientific one. He would not, for instance, have got lost in the whirlpool of debate over whether some scientist had told the truth about global warming.*

Ramakrishnan, Niranjan. *Reading Gandhi in the Twenty-First Century*. New York: Palgrave Macmillan, 2013. DOI: 10.1057/9781137325150.

DOI: 10.1057/978-1-137-32516-7

A strange paradox stalks our times. Everybody who's anybody in the business, political, or intellectual world, irrespective of country, is today a self-professed environmentalist. Simultaneously, the environment is slipping deeper into the abyss, faster than you can say "climate change."

The problem, self-evident to that fundamentalist Gandhi, is hidden from view by our own mythmaking. We insist we can somehow keep riding two horses at once, even if they are galloping in opposite directions. I'm calling Gandhi a fundamentalist in the sense that he never lost sight of the fundamentals. Nor was he ever afraid of the conclusions he might reach.

There is a memorable passage in Joseph Heller's *Catch-22*. Major Major Major is a mere private. The sergeant who conducts the daily drill is stern, harsh, and demanding, the way sergeants are expected to be. "I can beat the s**t out of any of you guys" is his frequent holler/boast/ threat during a parade. Then, one day, a computer with a sense of humor promotes Major Major Major to the rank of major. The very next day, the sergeant bellows, "Me and Major Major…can beat the s**t out of any of you guys."

A similar co-option has occurred in relation to the environment. Until a few decades ago, social and economic deprivation made possible the direct exploitation of human beings. The advances made by social movements and the liberation of traditionally labor-intensive countries resulted in the shutting off of many of the more egregious means of extracting human labor. Capitalism, as Gandhi noted while speaking of Henry Ford's mass-produced cars requires an endless supply of markets. It became necessary, as part of capitalist–industrial development, to co-opt previously untouched communities and nations into a new consumer universe. With the opening up of a huge segment of humanity—China, India, and Russia—to the consumer economy of the world in the past two decades, the only thing left for exploitation was the environment. Large tracts of forest and agricultural land were repurposed for commercial development, housing, malls, office space, or mines and factories. Artesian basins were freely polluted, as was the soil above. The middle classes of these countries were easily suborned, eager participants in the rush to turn every country into an America. As the poor in many of these countries suffered greatly, so too did the land, water, and air. And while the former could at least protest their plight, however feebly, the latter, being mute, needed human advocates to plead for them. These were hard to come by in a neoliberal environment in

DOI: 10.1057/978-1-137-32516-7

which everyone was sold on the idea of "development." Development and economic growth are now the twin mantras we live by, both held to be universal and sacrosanct.

Gandhi's approach to the environment was in keeping with his general philosophy. Perhaps the reason the quotation "Earth provides enough to satisfy every man's need, but not every man's greed"[1] is so often wrongly attributed to Mahatma Gandhi is that it seems so consonant with his philosophy. To Gandhi, taking more than one needed was theft, whether this was in relation to money, food, comfort, or even reading. An accumulative impulse was to him an impediment to an individual's liberation. A jail associate related how Gandhi insisted on reusing a twig to brush his teeth instead of plucking a new one each day.[2]

Gandhi's environmental sensitivities may also have had deeper origins in his personal life story. Though born into a strict vegetarian family, the young Gandhi started eating meat under the influence of a friend, even relishing it after some initial revulsion. He quit doing so after some months, but only because he had to eat in secret for fear of breaking his parents' hearts. He was convinced that meat was essential for good health and told himself that he would resume eating it after his parents had passed away and there was no longer any need for concealment.

This was the state of affairs when he left India to study law in England. His mother (his father having died) made him promise that he would not touch wine, women, or meat while he was abroad. During his time in England, the only item on which he came close to breaking his promise was the second. As for meat eating, Gandhi discovered philosophical vegetarianism accidentally when he came upon a vegetarian restaurant in London. The lad who had merely compelled himself to remain a vegetarian until his parents died now became a leading light of London's fledgling vegetarian community, a vegetarian of conviction, not upbringing.

Thus started a lifelong path of progressive self-denial. Not only of meat and eggs: he gave up root vegetables, coffee and tea, milk (later relenting and restricting his renunciation to cow's milk), spices, and salt. A sentience toward all life informed his outlook, as signified by the concept of *ahimsa* (literally, "non-hurting").

I mention these things at some length because the idea of limiting one's wants seems to me a missing element in the environmental movement. Some prominent writers and thinkers suggest that the key to tackling global warming, for example, is the adoption of nuclear power, just as

DOI: 10.1057/978-1-137-32516-7

others think the problem of air pollution by gas engines can be resolved by the electric car. Gandhi the fundamentalist would say the solution to such problems lay in giving up our mode of consuming recklessly and driving as though there were no tomorrow. The connection between individual sacrifice and society's problems was always central to Gandhi's approach.

How could anyone serious about the environment be simultaneously "pro-growth"? Telling the truth about the environment requires us to say that each point higher on the growth rate chart is another stake through the heart of the planet. Of course, no one who said this would have any hope of winning power—or retaining it. Gandhi said things like this because he had no fear of unpopularity. Even during his lifetime, in a country that suffered chronically from food shortages and where the Great Bengal Famine of 1943 was barely in the past, he criticized chemical fertilizers and compared them to poison:[3]

> There were people, remarked Gandhiji, who said that no basic reform in agriculture was possible without political power. They dreamt in terms of industrialization of agriculture by large-scale application of steam and electricity. He warned them that trading in soil fertility for the sake of quick returns would prove to be a disastrous, short-sighted policy. It would result in virtual depletion of the soil. Good earth called for the sweat of one's brow to yield the bread of life.
>
> People might criticize that approach as being slow and unprogressive. It did not hold out promise of dramatic results. Nevertheless, it held the key to the prosperity of both the soil and inhabitants living on it. Healthy, nourishing food was the alpha and omega of rural economy.

Gandhi was being consistent with something he had been saying all along:[4]

> God forbid that India should ever take to industrialism after the manner of the West. The economic imperialism of a single tiny island kingdom (England) is today keeping the world in chains. If an entire nation of 300 millions took to similar economic exploitation, it would strip the world bare like locusts.

That last phrase, "it would strip the world bare like locusts," may be read as a metaphor for colonialism, but as a statement about the environment it can be taken almost literally. The strip mining of coal and iron has turned an unbelievable number of "industrial" communities, from West Virginia to Eastern Europe, into human death traps and environmental

DOI: 10.1057/978-1-137-32516-7

hellholes. The current agitation in eastern India over a Korean conglomerate seeking to build a steel plant, and concerns about a London-based
corporation trying to buy a mountain with millions of tons of iron ore
buried underneath, reflect Gandhi's point. As does a 2012 article in the
*Smithsonian Magazine* reiterating the findings (popularly known as the
*Limits to Growth* report) of MIT computer models from 1972 that predicted a global economic collapse as a direct consequence of galloping
consumption resulting in the exhaustion of natural resources.[5] Gandhi's
instinctive sense, that a model of endless growth was unsustainable, is
being borne out both by news of water shortages in the daily papers and
in academic studies.

The subsuming of everything else in society to the economic "growth
rate" has meant lethal shortcuts and permanent damage to land, water,
and people. Professor Michael Nagler writes:

> The real purpose of an economic system is to guarantee to every person
> in its circle the fundamentals of physical existence (food, clothing, shelter)
> and the tools of meaningful work so that they can get on with the busi-
> ness of living together and working out our common destiny...By the
> time Gandhi's thinking on the subject matured in his classic treatise, *Hind
> Swaraj, or Indian Home Rule* (1909), he saw that our present economic system
> is being driven by a dangerous motive: the *multiplication of wants*. Because
> these wants are artificial—being that they created by advertising—and
> can never be satisfied, it creates what economist David Korten has called a
> "phantom economy" of fantastic financial manipulations that of course can
> never endure.[6]

That they cannot endure is true enough, just as hurricanes off the Florida
coast last no longer than a day or two. The damage they cause is no less
for that reason. The multiplication of wants that Nagler speaks about is a
direct concomitant of money from large industry, with advertising out-
lays that dwarf the national budgets of many a nation. With globalization,
its damage can reach the other end of the earth. The connection between
the rise in China's GDP, the corresponding increase in spending power,
the role of tiger body parts in traditional Chinese medicine, and the consequent impact on the Siberian and Indian tiger population, is a matter
of record. The flattening of hundreds of square miles of the rainforest to
grow fodder for cattle destined to figure in McDonald's "billions served"
is a direct consequence of the buying power of modern consumerism.

DOI: 10.1057/978-1-137-32516-7

The challenge facing the environmental movement is twofold. On the one hand, problems such as global warming are too large and too scientific to be conceived by the ordinary citizen, who has to accept someone else's word for whether it is happening, where, and how. On the other hand, there is a constant clamor for growth, and new forms of luxury and entertainment—not to mention perpetual upgrades to these. Unless the connection is made between a growing population, a population becoming addicted to economic growth, as evidenced by increasing consumption, and a planet turning increasingly into a wasteland, no real progress can be expected on this front.

Unless there are leaders who can step up and promise less growth and demand - and promise - less consumption, the problem can hardly be addressed. Talk of nuclear energy being "clean" is as self-delusional as naming a weapon that can destroy thousands a "Peacemaker." Unless so-called spiritual leaders lead by setting an example of minimal consumption instead of living the good life and preaching peace and harmony as they gad about on their chartered jets, a religion of simultaneous consumption and beatific virtue will do nothing to save either our temporal or our spiritual abode.

Gandhi's words from *Hind Swaraj* apply to many topics in this book, not least the environment: "Hinduism, Islam, Zoroastrianism, Christianity and all other religions teach that we should remain passive about worldly pursuits..., that we should set a limit to our worldly ambitions and that our religious ambition should be illimitable. Our activity should be directed into the latter channel."[7]

Unless we confront this basic dichotomy directly, as Gandhi did, rejecting industrialization, particularly big industry, recognizing the siren song of economic growth for what it is, and wising up to the seductions of consumerism, we will continue to be misled by the mirage that somehow we can luxuriate our way to environmental homeostasis.

# Notes

1   The words actually belong to Frank Buchman, founder of Moral Rearmament.
2   The Eco-Friendly Toothbrush blog, quoting from Kaka Kalelkar, *Stray Glimpses of Bapu*, Ahmedabad, Navajivan Publication House [1950] (http://www. gandhitopia.org/profiles/blogs/the-eco-friendly-tooth-brush).

DOI: 10.1057/978-1-137-32516-7

3  "Speech at Industries Ministers' Conference", *Collected Works of Mahatma Gandhi*, Vol. 91, p. 389.
4  "Discussion with a Capitalist", *Collected Works of Mahatma Gandhi*, Vol. 43, pp. 412–413.
5  *Young India*, December 20, 1928.
6  Michael Nagler, "Economic Crisis or Nonviolent Opportunity? Gandhi's Answer to Financial Collapse," August 2011 (http://wagingnonviolence. org/2011/08/economic-crisis-or-nonviolent-opportunity-gandhis-answer-to-financial-collapse/) (emphasis in original).
7  *Hind Swaraj*.

DOI: 10.1057/978-1-137-32516-7

# 7
# The C(l)ash of Civilizations

Abstract: *In the early 1990s, the Stanford scholar Francis Fukuyama declared that history was at an end, now that the Cold War had been won. Yet strife and bloodshed have continued unabated, if not increased. Gandhi might have pointed out to Fukuyama that peace was not a matter of ideology, and that Western economic models premised on human greed were wedded rather inextricably to violence.*

Ramakrishnan, Niranjan. *Reading Gandhi in the Twenty-First Century.* New York: Palgrave Macmillan, 2013.
DOI: 10.1057/9781137325150.

*The one-l lama,*
*He's a priest.*
*The two-l llama,*
*He's a beast.*

—Ogden Nash, "The Lama"

In 1993, *Foreign Affairs* magazine published a now famous article, "The Clash of Civilizations," written by Professor Samuel Huntington of Harvard. The burden of Huntington's thesis, soon to be expanded into a full-length book with the same title, was simple and seductive. With the end of the Cold War, he argued, the era of ideological conflicts had come to a close; the geopolitical fault lines had changed. In the twenty-first century ideology would take a back seat to identity. And identity, contended Huntington, would thereafter be predominantly civilizational, defining civilization as the largest human grouping short of the completely generic term "human."

> In class and ideological conflicts, the key question was "Which side are you on?" and people could and did choose sides and change sides. In conflicts between civilizations, the question is "What are you?" That is a given that cannot be changed.[1]

A couple of years before Huntington's article was published, Senator Daniel Patrick Moynihan of the US Congress had given a talk in Europe. Laden with foreboding, it expressed a mood that was also to be reflected in a book arising out of his lecture. *Pandemonium* predicted the rise of ethnicity in the coming decades as a major force in world affairs. As the book coincided with the unraveling of the Soviet Union in 1991, with Yugoslavia following suit in a much bloodier second act, Moynihan's views also seemed prescient.

Renowned as they were for their originality, both Huntington and Moynihan would have happily conceded that they were not saying something entirely novel. They had merely extended to the world scale something that others, perhaps with a smaller megaphone, had expressed before. Students of Indian history will be familiar—many who lived through the times painfully so—with names such as Sarvarkar and Jinnah, prophets who proclaimed similar visions, albeit on a purely Indian firmament. The former said:

> We Hindus are bound together not only by the love we bear to a common fatherland and by the blood that courses through our veins...but also by

DOI: 10.1057/978-1-137-32516-7

the tie of the common homage we pay to our great civilisation—our Hindu culture.... [W]e are one because we are a nation, a race and own a common Sanskriti [civilisation].[2]

Echoing Sarvarkar, Jinnah declared that Muslims and Hindus were "Two Nations," and demanded a separate homeland for Muslims in the subcontinent. The fault lines he propounded were not ethnic but religious, cultural, civilizational:

> The Hindus and Muslims belong to two different religious philosophies, social customs, litterateurs. They neither intermarry nor interdine together and, indeed, they belong to two different civilizations which are based mainly on conflicting ideas and conceptions. Their aspect on life and of life are different. It is quite clear that Hindus and Mussalmans derive their inspiration from different sources of history. They have different epics, different heroes, and different episodes. Very often the hero of one is a foe of the other and, likewise, their victories and defeats overlap. To yoke together two such nations under a single state, one as a numerical minority and the other as a majority, must lead to growing discontent and final destruction of any fabric that may be so built for the government of such a state.[3]

But shared religious background appears to offer no guarantee of harmony either. For much of the late twentieth century Irish Protestants and Catholics were tearing apart Northern Ireland. The Shia–Sunni bloodletting in Iraq post-Saddam, the anti-Shia bombings in Pakistan, and the crushing of Sunnis in Syria and of Shias in Bahrain belong to the recent past if not the actual present. And we can also mention the ongoing plight of the Ahmadis in Pakistan.

Then there is caste. In post-independence India, with a well-established electoral system providing "official" levers to power, pelf, and patronage, caste conflict has riven a wide and growing number of regions, its impacts ranging from routine political jockeying to pitched battles and bloodshed.

Indian political writers from Sarvarkar to Lohia have lamented how caste consciousness dominates the Indian psyche, overshadowing other (and in their view, more desirable) potential contenders, including nation, race, even civilization. It is hard to resist this brief fictional exchange in which the recently departed satirist and author Shrilal Shukla captured it all so well:

> "Who are you, brother?"

DOI: 10.1057/978-1-137-32516-7

Every Indian has just one easy answer to this question and that is to promptly say the name of his caste. So he said, "I'm an Aggarwal."[4]

And long before Sarvarkar or Jinnah, even longer before Huntington and Moynihan, a famous refugee from Germany had proclaimed another division in society, this one based on class. Going one step further, he also declared the inevitability of a class struggle, a violent one. While the validity of his prognostications was called into question by the happenings and non-happenings of the century that followed, Marx's emphasis on the role class plays in shaping human consciousness has endured splendidly.

The authors of all these theories would likely allow that multiple "consciousnesses" can and do simultaneously inhabit a person's head and heart. There is little doubt that the complexities of individual and collective behaviors, and the sources within the psyche which shape them, will continue to provide employment to sociologists and political scientists for a long time. To paraphrase Marx, sociologists have hitherto told us of the various schisms in society; the point, however, is to bridge them.

Two astute observers of humanity, Mark Twain and George Bernard Shaw, held poverty to be the real dividing line, and saw enrichment as the way out of human strife. Playing on the biblical saying "The love of money is the root of all evil," Mark Twain quipped that the *lack* of money was the root of all evil. Bernard Shaw, most notably in *Major Barbara*, rubbished the disdain for money and extolled its virtues:

> Money is the most important thing in the world. It represents health, strength, honor, generosity and beauty as conspicuously and undeniably as the want of it represents illness, weakness, disgrace, meanness and ugliness. Not the least of its virtues is that it destroys base people as certainly as it fortifies and dignifies noble people. It is only when it is cheapened to worthlessness for some, and made impossibly dear to others, that it becomes a curse. In short, it is a curse only in such foolish social conditions that life itself is a curse. For the two things are inseparable: Money is the counter that enables life to be distributed socially: it is life as truly as sovereigns and bank notes are money.[5]

In a later work, *Pygmalion*, Shaw extended the role of money to include underpinning the very morals of society. Looked at another way, the numerous kinds of consciousness, if we consider them to be notions of ourselves, require money to sustain them.

In the Marxist view, classes would, over the course of time, disappear of their own accord in a post-communist society. We need not linger

DOI: 10.1057/978-1-137-32516-7

here to explore the endless intra-Marxist squabbles over whether it was feasible to have "true" communism in a single country, other than to note that in Marxist eyes the class struggle continues on an international scale between the communist and the non-communist universes. A practically identical view obtains among many ideologues of Islam, which traditionally divides the world into Dar-ul Islam (House of Islam, i.e., peace) and Dar-ul Harb (House of War). The doctrine of inevitable success, too, is common to both ideologies. Where conversion of the "other" is either seen as impossible or deemed unnecessary, societies have tried a slew of techniques, from subjugation to marginalization, all the way to outright ethnic cleansing or genocide. Propositional countries such as Israel and Pakistan have attempted to construct an artificial structure where a certain race or religion would dominate.

Gandhi rejected all of these solutions. Unlike Twain or Shaw, he did not see money as a panacea, although, like Shaw, he did see work as the essential element of life. Equally, he did not visualize an India that would be all one religion or another, just as he did not see eye to eye with many of his own followers who were convinced caste must be abolished. His main criticism of Islam was its quickness to violence,[6] just as his principal disagreement with communism was its emphasis upon the same.[7] Though communism advocated ends that broadly resonated with him, he did think it fanciful to imagine a world without any economic inequality, saying that "the rich and the poor will always be with us."[8] In all this, Gandhi, usually considered the textbook utopian, turns out to be every bit the hard-headed realist, happy to countenance a world of human beings with a disparity of skills, wealth—and ideas.

"What men say matters to me not too much; what they do matters a lot," Rammanohar Lohia once told an American audience.[9] For Gandhi, whatever consciousness drove a human being, what counted was how he acted. It was clear to him early on that it was in this context that the word "civilization" must be understood: "Civilization is that mode of conduct which points out to man the path of duty. Performance of duty and observance of morality are convertible terms. To observe morality is to attain mastery over our mind and our passions. So doing, we know ourselves."

This quotation is from the chapter "What Is True Civilization?" in *Hind Swaraj*.[10] In our current context of dealing with the "other," the word "civilization" here can be replaced with any of the many fault lines: ethnicity, religion, race, caste, political persuasion, and so on. In typical fashion,

DOI: 10.1057/978-1-137-32516-7

Gandhi asks a simple question that gets to the heart of the matter: "If *You* are a European/Muslim/Brahmin/Aryan/..., what does your action say about *You*?" The biblical injunction that "by their fruits ye shall know them" was Gandhi's test. With this as a standard he could appeal to any section, for he was calling upon the individual to live up to the highest ideals in the individual's own belief system.

I suspect the hard-headed *bania*[11] in Gandhi instinctively grasped a central reality: social conflict, though cloaked in caste, religious, civilizational, or some fancy sociological garb, ultimately boiled down to the basest human motives. In *zar, zan, zamin*, as the Punjabi proverb has it, lies the origin of all strife.[12] And working on this divide in the human (yes, that grouping right above Huntington's civilizational grouping) heart, one might say, was the Mahatma's master key.

Gandhi rejected a model based on human greed, which he saw even in ostensibly anticapitalist paradigms from the West:

> Socialism and communism of the West are based on certain conceptions...fundamentally different from ours. One such conception is their belief in the essential selfishness of human nature. I do not subscribe to it, for I know that the essential difference between man and the brute is that the former can respond to the call of the spirit in him, can rise superior to the passions that he owns in common with the brute and, therefore, superior to selfishness and violence, which belong to the brute nature and not to the immortal spirit of man.[13]

Echoing something he had written decades before in *Hind Swaraj*,[14] Gandhi continues:

> That is the fundamental conception of Hinduism, which has years of penance and austerity at the back of the discovery of their [*sic*] truth. That is why whilst we had had saints who have burnt out their bodies and laid down their lives in order to explore the secrets of the soul, we have none as in the West who have laid down their lives in exploring the remotest or highest regions of earth. Our socialism or communism should therefore be based on non-violence and on the harmonious co-operation of labour and capital and the landlord and the tenant.

Alone among the leaders of the modern world, Gandhi disdained the formula of steering the populace away from internecine strife with promises of "development," the universally applied technique of bribing with baubles, if you will. A quick look will tell us how common this is. In Gandhi's own land, India, there are more cell phones than working

DOI: 10.1057/978-1-137-32516-7

toilets, even as a child malnutrition rate worse than that of sub-Saharan Africa rubs shoulders with a booming gourmet food industry. The first thing that the government of Saudi Arabia did upon the breakout of the Arab Spring of 2011 was to settle a couple of thousand dollars on each citizen. Cheap imports and a series of artificial bubbles have kept Americans quiescent for several decades, even as American society continues to break down in a variety of ways. This was also how the late Colonel Gaddafi kept the various tribes and regions in Libya from being at each other's throats, with oil revenues going to subsidize creature comforts.

Another way of bridging these various divisions is to point to a common enemy outside. The well-honed Pakistani technique of raising the Indian bogeyman on the slightest pretext is an example. For decades the Saudis defused dangers to the kingdom from Wahhabi enthusiasms by sending thousands of young men and millions of riyals in aid of mini-jihads abroad. The "communist threat" kept American politics simple and safe from fissiparous trends for half a century.

To Gandhi, it would appear, there was no clever artifice around divides other than transcending them. The two standard conventional solutions above were both closed to him. As a well-known opponent of development and industrialism, the option of holding out a future consumer paradise overflowing with milk and honey to distract men and women raring to go at their enemies was ruled out. Obviously, the path of stoking hatred against some third group to paper over internal divides was anathema. What was left, then, and with an almost Sherlockian clarity,[15] was a simple solution, though, as with most of Gandhi's prescriptions, perhaps not an easy one.

The root of the problem lay in human greed, and therefore the problem would not be solved by promoting more greed. It could not be addressed other than temporarily by amusing the masses with entertainment or trinkets (gadgets in our day). The only hope, as Gandhi saw it, lay in the inherent strength of Indian civilization: a long and hoary tradition of self-restraint. Gandhi's solution to the vicissitudes of humanity was inseparable from an economic, political—and, indeed, spiritual—shift in perspective:

> A man should consider himself not the owner of his property but its trustee
> or custodian. He will use it for the service of society. He will accept only
> that much for himself as he has earned with his labour. If that happens,
> no one will be poor and no one rich. In such a system all religions will

DOI: 10.1057/978-1-137-32516-7

naturally be held equal. Therefore all quarrels arising out of religions, caste and economic differences will be ended.[16]

In Gandhi's conception, goodwill toward one's neighbors, tolerance, and the readiness to suffer in the hope of opening another's eyes ought to provide assurance enough to live among others, no matter of what race, caste, religion, ideology, or ethnicity.

It was a formulation that could be applied to international relations as well. It is fashionable for many these days to trumpet that throughout its history India had never attacked others, even though it has been invaded times without number. Oddly enough, these are often the same people who favor endless armament and clamor for an invasion of Pakistan any time a stray cracker goes off anywhere in India. Gandhi, by contrast, actually believed in this putative Indian virtue:

> Since we shall be at peace with all the rest of the world, neither exploiting, nor being exploited, we should have the smallest army imaginable. This is the India of my dreams....
>
> Indeed, I believe that Independent India can only discharge her duty towards a groaning world by adopting a simple but ennobled life by developing her thousands of cottage [industries] and living at peace with the world. High thinking is inconsistent with complicated material life based on high speed imposed on us by Mammon worship. All the graces of life are possible only when we learn the art of living nobly.[17]

Looking at geopolitics over the past 2,000 years, we can allow that limitless greed drove the European powers to colonial expansion, however much they may have proclaimed, and sometimes even believed, that there was a higher purpose at work. As the economic journalist Garet Garrett noted sixty years ago, there is a barely discernible line, crossing which nations tip over from republic into empire, with some grandiose delusion assisting each such transition: "The Roman Empire never doubted that it was the defender of civilization. Its good intentions were peace, law and order. The Spanish Empire added salvation. The British Empire added the noble myth of the white man's burden. We [the USA] have added freedom and democracy."[18]

Thus it was, if less burdened by ideology, with the litany of invasions in India's history, when kings and adventurers alike periodically burst across the Khyber Pass. Battling the infidels no doubt figured somewhere, but visions of a fabled land of gold and diamonds were hardly absent from their considerations. Indeed, given that there was Muslim

DOI: 10.1057/978-1-137-32516-7

rule in Delhi from 1193 AD, all subsequent invasions from Afghanistan, Persia, or Central Asia were presumably driven by the lure of loot, and not by any imperative to spread the Word. On a different continent, an old joke from Apartheid-era South Africa tells the same story: "When the white man came, he had the Book [Bible] and we had the land. Now he has the land, and we have the Book!"

E. F. Schumacher once spoke of Gandhi looking askance at notions of systems so perfect that no one would have to be good. In a sense, Gandhi was only echoing a sentiment expressed much earlier by a veteran of the American Revolution, who too thought that it was not treaties and constitutions that would determine whether we could keep the peace, but the nature of man himself:

> We have no government armed with power capable of contending with human passions unbridled by morality and religion. Avarice, ambition, revenge, or gallantry, would break the strongest cords of our Constitution as a whale goes through a net. Our Constitution was made only for a moral and religious people. It is wholly inadequate to the government of any other.[19]

# Notes

1   Samuel Huntington, "The Clash of Civilizations," *Foreign Affairs*, Summer 1993.
2   V. D. Savarkar, *Hindutva—Who Is a Hindu?*, Veer Savarkar Prakashan, 1969.
3   Mohammed Ali Jinnah, presidential address to the All India Muslim League, Lahore, March 22, 1940.
4   Shrilal Shukla, *Raag Darbari*, Translated in English by Gillian Wright, Penguin Books, 1992, p. 275.
5   George Bernard Shaw, preface, *Major Barbara*, Brentano's, 1907.
6   "The sword is no emblem of Islam. But Islam was born in an environment where the sword was, and still remains, the supreme law. ... The sword is yet too much in evidence among the Mussalmas. It must be sheathed if Islam is to be what it means-peace" (*Young India*, December 30, 1926).
7   "All that I know is that [Bolshevism] aims at the abolition of the institution of private property. This is only an application of the ethical ideal of non-possession in the realm of economics and if the people adopted this ideal of their own accord or could be made to accept it by means of peaceful persuasion, there would be nothing like it. But from what I know of Bolshevism, it not only does not preclude the use of force, but freely sanctions it for the expropriation of private property and maintaining the Collective

DOI: 10.1057/978-1-137-32516-7

State ownership of the same. And if that is so, I have no hesitation in saying that the Bolshevik regime in its present form cannot last for long. For it is my firm conviction that nothing enduring can be built on violence" (*Young India*, November 15, 1928).

8    "The rich and the poor will always be with us. But their mutual relations will be subject to Constant change. France is a republic, but there are all classes of men in France" (*Young India*, January 8, 1925).

9    Harris Wofford, Jr., *Lohia and America Meet*, Sindhu Publications, 1987.

10   *Collected Works of Mahatma Gandhi*, Vol. 10, p. 279.

11   Gandhi, who was born into the caste of Modh Bania, or grocers, often poked fun at himself over the reputed greed and hard-headed business mentality of the trader. For example, "There are people who may call me a visionary but I tell you I am a real bania and my business is to obtain swaraj" (speech to the All India Congress Committee, August 7, 1942, *Collected Works of Mahatma Gandhi*, Vol. 83, p. 185) or "I am not likely to be lured by your logic. After all I am a Bania, am I not?" (talk with C. Rajagopalachari, *Collected Works of Mahatma Gandhi*, Vol. 95, p. 138).

12   *Har qatl di e jar, zan, zameen ya zar* ("The root of every killing—woman, land or gold").

13   Interview with *The Pioneer* newspaper of Lucknow, published on August 3, 1934; reproduced in *Collected Works of Mahatma Gandhi*, Vol. 64, pp. 231–232.

14   See full quotation in Chapter 3.

15   "How often have I said to you that when you have eliminated the impossible, whatever remains, however improbable, must be the truth?" (A. Conan Doyle, *The Sign of Four*, Spencer Blackett, 1890).

16   Foreword, "Varnavyavastha," May 31, 1945; reproduced in *Collected Works of Mahatma Gandhi*, Vol. 87, p. 24.

17   "Alternative to Industrialization", *Harijan*, January 1, 1946; reproduced in *Collected Works of Mahatma Gandhi*, Vol. 92, p. 63.

18   Garet Garrett, *The American Empire*, Caxton Printers, 1952.

19   *The Works of John Adams*, ed. C. F. Adams, Little, Brown, 1851, Vol. 4, p. 31.

DOI: 10.1057/978-1-137-32516-7

# 8

# East versus West: Win, Lose, or Draw?

Abstract: *So what happened when Kipling was proven wrong, and the twain did end up meeting? The East is rising, registering economic growth rates that are the envy of the West. Having fallen on uncertain times and no longer sure of itself, the West appears confused about its own values. In this apparent spirit of new influence, is each side throwing its baby out with the bath water? A view of Gandhi and the challenges of multiculturalism.*

Ramakrishnan, Niranjan. *Reading Gandhi in the Twenty-First Century*. New York: Palgrave Macmillan, 2013. DOI: 10.1057/9781137325150.

A famous actress, the story goes, once suggested marriage to George Bernard Shaw. With his brains and her looks, she reasoned, their children would be both brilliant and beautiful. GBS demurred: what if the offspring ended up with her brains and his looks?[1]

The encounter of the past quarter-century between East and West might be viewed in a somewhat similar light, and not only by cynics. Anyone watching developments over the past few decades might regard Rudyard Kipling's line "East is East and West is West, and never the twain shall meet" as quaint, if not hopelessly wrong.

That time was on the move, even in lands where antiquity seemed to travel along with the present, was a sentiment often expressed by anti-colonial leaders in the mid-twentieth century, even though the labors involved in the transition to modernity must have seemed Sisyphean. "He who tries to predict the India of tomorrow would be a bold man," India's first prime minister, Jawaharlal Nehru, is said to have remarked, adding, "He who would predict the India of the next century would be a mad man." With that "next" century well underway and India's resurgence on every lip as the country is projected to become one of the world's three largest economies, it is time to revisit Nehru's answer.

His words could equally have applied to China, another "midnight's child," which began its modern-day journey at about the same time as its southern neighbor. Ancient civilizations both, coming into their own after centuries of European exploitation, they promised to provide a unique laboratory for testing a longstanding question: "What determines a society's destiny—nature or culture?"

The debate has drawn several authors, with two famous books presenting opposite sides of the argument: Jared Diamond's *Guns, Germs and Steel* and David Landes' *The Wealth and Poverty of Nations: Why Some Are So Rich and Others So Poor*. Both were published in the late 1990s.

Diamond's bestseller sought to demolish notions of any inherent European supremacy, attributing Europe's rise to a few basic divergences in the way Providence scattered her riches—things as mundane as gaining an early immunity to livestock diseases, the kinds of wildlife native to various lands, the varieties of crops that could be sustained ... And the mastery of gun making by Europe would seal the fates of its opponents.

Landes' book sought to refute this thesis, arguing that factors such as climate and soil alone could not explain the European surge of the past 500 years. For one thing, the development of a counterweight in

DOI: 10.1057/978-1-137-32516-7

society to religious/shamanist obscurantism or imperial caprice seems a giant point of difference between European societies and others. Part of this cultural makeover, according to Landes, is an increased tolerance of criticism and an innate fostering of debate and experiment—a good mix of innovation, adaptation, and forbearance being a distinctive feature of the European mindscape.

What does the past sixty years of Chinese and Indian history say about these two theses? Although Diamond's view appears relevant for large parts of the world, including the equatorial regions, Africa and Latin America, his thesis seems less applicable to China and India, both agricultural exponents of long standing, and (India in particular) blessed with an astonishing variety of flora and fauna.

A popular chart making the email rounds shows the relative contributions of various countries to world GDP over the past two centuries. In 1820, India contributed around 18 percent and China around 32 percent; the United States came in at around 3 percent. By the 1950s, the United States was up around 27 percent, while India and China hovered at around 5 percent each. In 2001, the figures were roughly 21 percent for the United States, 12 percent for China, and 6 percent for India.

Even though global GDP contribution is far from being the sole measure of a country's well-being, the question of how China and India went from providing 50 percent of humanity's goods and services in 1820 to a mere 10 percent in 1950 bears examination. It could be argued that the speed of this decline is as much an indication of the frailties of Chinese and Indian society at the time as it is of the pioneering spirit of the West (or its rapacity).

Are China's and India's societies so different today than in the past that their economic supremacy is all but assured, as we keep hearing? It is common to cite the cleaning lady with her cell phone as a metaphor for a changed milieu. But it is equally noteworthy that state-of-the-art gadgetry does nothing to increase respect for the law, solicitude for the rights of others, or consideration for the commons, all of which are more genuine indices of a culture than its technical accoutrements. China has its own stories of forced evictions, partymen running side-businesses, and sundry *jiski lathi uski bhains* ("he who holds the stick gets the buffalo") tales of woe.

Comes an impatient answer: during such an epic transition, surely you can overlook a few heads being broken! Both countries have in their vision some replica of the consumer heaven they see in the West.

DOI: 10.1057/978-1-137-32516-7

Time alone will tell how it all shakes out, but one thing is for sure: there seems to be very little that is original in the works, just a patina of Western mores, tinsel, and catchphrases slapped on top of a basically unaltered ethos of feudalism (in India) and totalitarianism (in China), with proponents firm in their belief that the paint will eventually transmute the structure underneath. Seep-down economics, if you will.

Rammanohar Lohia, the Indian freedom fighter and socialist ideologue, wrote that the twentieth century had produced one originator, Mahatma Gandhi, and one discovery, the atom bomb.[2] To recast Lohia's words for today: there is one invention, the globalized consumer, and the same innovator, Mahatma Gandhi. In *Hind Swaraj*, Gandhi seeks to address a simple but profound question: "Is a utopia predicated on unending material fulfillment ever possible, even leaving aside its desirability?" It is a question a rising West with low populations, plenty of land, and colonies galore did not have to ask, especially since "consumption" then was quite literally a dreaded word. It is a question the two Himalayan giants of today have sidelined in their hurry to "catch up." Unfortunately it is a question that will not disappear with the icecaps.

Something that does seem to be disappearing, meanwhile, is some of that ethos that Landes identified as embodying the winning specialties of the Western world. Free speech, defined with the broadest latitude to include the freedom to give offense, has received severe setbacks over the past decade in America, and for longer perhaps in Europe. "Multiculturalism," the new watchword generally connoting a need to avoid controversy at all costs, is frequently on elite lips in the West. And each time the dust settles following any imbroglio over a supposed breach of multicultural etiquette, there seems to be a little less freedom of expression around than there was before, and a little more circumspection over whether it is worth the trouble to speak one's mind.

In the 2005 Mohammed cartoons controversy is laid bare one real cost of globalization: Western ideals in hock to the lure of free trade. The same people who are willing to start wars 8,000 miles away in the name of democracy are ready to water it down at home at the first sign of economic disruption emanating from faraway lands. The global chickens have come home to roost. The question is whether the West will defend the central pillar of the Enlightenment or abandon it to the

DOI: 10.1057/978-1-137-32516-7

new faith of "getting along at any price" mealy-mouthed obeisance to self-censorship in the name of multiculturalism. Will it defend the one thing that has distinguished life in the West from life elsewhere on the planet: the protected freedom of expression? Or will it surrender before the threat of Danish biscuits vanishing from Arab store shelves?

The signs are not encouraging. After the Danish prime minister explained politely to critics that the government in Denmark could not control the press, some EU high-up weighed in with a disingenuous statement about the need to be sensitive to religion and culture. Following bravely were luminaries such as Kofi Annan, who sullied his post by watching mutely while a UN member state was savaged in a premeditated war, now expostulating on the need for freedom of the press to be tempered by respect for religion. Not to be left behind was the US Department of State, whose spokeswoman blasted the Danish and other European papers for publishing the cartoons, stressing the need for press responsibility.

The assault on free speech has been happening on a smaller scale for some time. I recall the time when a company in the United States used a picture of Gandhi in some unflattering fashion. A howl of protest went up on the Internet, and the company folded with the usual noises of forced apology and assurances of how much it respected the great man, et cetera, et cetera. Some years back a play had to be canceled in the United Kingdom because some members of the Sikh faith felt it offended them. The British state was nowhere about to protect the right of the organizers. (In fact, the playwright, I recall reading, had to hide in fear of death threats. Not all are as prominent as Salman Rushdie.)

To stress Gandhi's credentials as a believer in communal tolerance would be akin to emphasizing that the earth is round. Gandhi not only believed it was possible for various communities to coexist peacefully, but quite literally in the end laid down his life for his efforts to forge a peace between the communities.

Less known are his attitudes toward opposing opinions. Rammanohar Lohia spoke of the time when he requested Gandhi to write for a journal he was bringing out. After reading some past issues, Gandhi said to Lohia, "You must never expect me to write because you don't appear to have the slightest patience with your opponent's viewpoint."[3] Lohia also wrote of how free one felt in Gandhi's presence, of how even someone who was a fraction of the Mahatma's age could speak his or her mind

DOI: 10.1057/978-1-137-32516-7

to him. It was Gandhi who said, in response to Rabindranath Tagore's apprehensions about the whiff of narrow nationalism in his statements against the use of English:

> I hope I am as great a believer in free air as the great Poet. I do not want my house to be walled in on all sides and my windows to be stuffed. I want the cultures of all the lands to be blown about my house as freely as possible. But I refuse to be blown off my feet by any.[4]

Nevertheless, many have observed that Gandhi was rather ruthless in response to challenges to his leadership. They cite his connivance in the undermining of Subhas Chandra Bose in the late 1930s, when the latter was rising as a popular leader among the country's youth. Others look askance at his apparent indifference to the execution of Bhagat Singh, a national hero at twenty-three for his courage and the inspiration he offered.

Early into his Indian phase after his return from South Africa, Gandhi found himself addressing accusations of autocracy, ironically, in the context of his opposition to his party's demand that the British prosecute an English general who had overseen the Jallianwala Bagh massacre:

> I have often been charged with having an unyielding nature. I have been told that I would not bow to the decision of the majority. I have been accused of being autocratic....On the contrary I pride myself on my yielding nature in non-vital matters. I detest autocracy. Valuing my freedom and independence I equally cherish them for others. I have no desire to carry a single soul with me, if I cannot appeal to his or her reason.[5]

And befitting one who went by the spirit rather than the letter, he added in the same breath:

> But I have found by experience that if I wish to live in society and still retain my independence, I must limit the points of utter independence to matters of first rate importance. In all others which do not involve a departure from one's personal religion or moral code, one must yield to the majority.

My own understanding of Gandhi's stance is as follows: Gandhi felt the national movement had to be clear and unambiguous about its commitment to nonviolence. Any wavering on his part on this issue would confuse public opinion and give a fillip to means that, even though they might seem efficacious in the short run, would cause enormous trouble down the road.

DOI: 10.1057/978-1-137-32516-7

In the matter of expression, on the other hand, there is a long record of Gandhi being not only tolerant but even cordial toward those diametrically opposed to his views, and even those who were vituperative in their denunciations. His critics spanned a wide range, including Hindu and Muslim fanatics, respectable versions of the same, communists, sections of the Indian elite, separatists such as Periyar E. V. Ramasami Naicker and B. R. Ambedkar, not to mention Gandhi-hating English among the planter class and officialdom. I am not aware of any instance of Gandhi trying to suppress the writings of others, proponents or antagonists, or seeking to have anyone arrested, or in any way harrassed, for expressing any view.

The touchstone of Gandhi's approach was tolerance and forbearance. Some time ago I came across a pristine statement made by Gandhi long before the days of communal chaos around the time of partition: "I don't expect the India of my dreams... to be wholly Hindu, or wholly Christian, or wholly Mussalman, but I want it to be wholly tolerant..."[6] In *Hind Swaraj* he speaks of the secret of Indian civilization lying in its fostering of self-restraint. Gandhi's own moderation in speech and criticism would point to his having imbibed this lesson. Bringing round an opponent required, in Gandhi's view, changing the former's heart, a task made a thousand times more difficult if one succumbed to provocation and insulted or demeaned him.

It was an elemental part of Gandhi's makeup not only to listen to the other side, but to make sure that it received full and fair representation in his own argument. Even when the charge was malicious or unfair, he would consider its merits and seek any little truth it might bear, as his article "A Lesson from the Plague,"[7] written in 1904 for *Indian Opinion*, demonstrates. A better example of the contrast between Gandhi's approach to calumny and the routine umbrage that accompanies the slightest hint of criticism in our politically correct era would be hard to find:

> We have a homely saying in India that it were better for a man to lose millions than[8] that he should lose a good name. It follows as a corollary from the saying that, once a man has acquired a bad name, it is difficult for him to undo the effect and to rehabilitate himself in the popular regard. What is true of individuals is equally true of communities. The French have a name for the artistic, the English for personal bravery, the Germans for hard-headedness, the Russians for frugality, the Colonies in

DOI: 10.1057/978-1-137-32516-7

South Africa for gold hunger; similarly, the Indians in South Africa have, rightly or wrongly, got the evil reputation of being insanitary and ignorant of the first principles of hygiene. The result is that the individual members against whom such a charge could not be proved to the slightest extent are often obliged to undergo hardships merely because they belong to the Indian community. Nor could it be otherwise....

Such regulations,[9] harsh as they undoubtedly are, ought not to make us angry. But we should so order our conduct as to prevent a repetition of them. And with that end in view, we should set about putting our houses in order as well literally as figuratively. The meanest of us should know the value of sanitation and hygiene. Overcrowding should be stamped out from our midst. We should freely let in sunshine and air. In short, we should ingrain into our hearts the English saying that cleanliness is next to godliness.

In contrast to the clamors of "My group/religion/community is owed respect" in our times, for Gandhi, respect and reputation are earned, not demanded. He continues:

And what then? We do not promise that we shall at once be freed from the yoke of prejudice. A name once lost is not to be so easily regained. The loss of a name is like a disease, it overtakes us in no time, but it costs us much to remove. But why need we think of reward in the shape of sub-sidence of prejudice? Is not cleanliness its own reward? Would it not be an inestimable boon to ward off another attack of the plague? Would we not cease to be harassed by sanitary inspectors and their regulations in that they will have lost their use? By and by, when we have asserted our position as a people regarding sanitation and hygiene as part of our being, and not merely of lip profession, the prejudice, in so far as it is based on that charge, will go.

A persuasive case could be made that free India's democracy and freedoms were a direct result of the nature of Gandhi's movement. As independence approached, Gandhi surprised and sometimes outraged close colleagues by insisting that some talented individuals who had not only opposed the freedom movement but even abused him personally should be taken into the cabinet or given other responsibilities so that the country might not be deprived of their skills and services.

Unlike the West, which is now contending with the new experience of having large numbers of people from multiple religions and cultures,

DOI: 10.1057/978-1-137-32516-7

India had been home for people from practically every part of the "known world" for centuries before Gandhi. Gandhi himself spent his early years in a coastal town inhabited by people of different religions and backgrounds. Partly because of this exposure, partly owing to his staying in cosmopolitan England while still in his teens, and immeasurably due to his leadership of the Indian community in South Africa, comprising Hindus, Muslims, Sikhs, and Christians, Tamils, Gujaratis, North Indians, and more, Gandhi had firsthand experience of living and working together with diverse populations. He realized that a great deal of tolerance, huge amounts of self-restraint, and not least a sense of humor were essential in such an endeavour.

In the decades leading up to the twenty-first century there was a huge population transfer from East to West (or South to North), and a transfer of wealth in the opposite direction (news of the BRIC countries proposing to bail out the Euro zone sets the seal on this development). What have these transfers brought? The East draws approving cheers for its newfound energy and acquisitiveness. The West seems to be foundering on its own shibboleths of free trade and political correctness, while letting go of its rule of law and Enlightenment freedoms. What seems to unite both is an unbridled consumer culture that is raping the earth.

"Let us fear God and we shall cease to fear Man," said Gandhi.[8] We are embarked upon exactly the opposite course, committing horrendous crimes against man and beast alike while treading carefully to avoid any likely charge of unfashionable language or etiquette.

# Notes

1   This response might not have been altogether tongue-in-cheek. George Bernard Shaw was a serious proponent of evolving a race of supermen through the use of eugenics.

2   Rammanohar Lohia, *Marx, Gandhi and Socialism*, Navhind, 1963, p. 245.

3   Rammanohar Lohia, *Marx, Gandhi and Socialism*, Navhind, 1963, p. 144.

4   *Collected Works of Mahatma Gandhi*, Vol. 23, p. 215.

5   *Collected Works of Mahatma Gandhi*, Vol. 21, p. 45.

6   *Young India*, December 22, 1927.

7   *Collected Works of Mahatma Gandhi*, Vol. 3, pp. 481–482.

DOI: 10.1057/978-1-137-32516-7

8   "We have a homely saying in India that it were better for a man to lose millions then that he should lose a good name" taken from *Collected Works of Mahatma Gandhi* where "than" was misspelt as "then."

9   Regulation here refers to the plague regulations against Indians.

10  *Speeches and Writings of Mahatma Gandhi*, 4th edition, Madras: G. A. Natesan & Co., 1933, p. 130.

DOI: 10.1057/978-1-137-32516-7

# 9

# Media Matters... *and Citizen Mutters*

Abstract: *Nowhere is the everyday impact of technology felt more than in the sophistication of mass media. At no time has the average citizen been so deluged by information, nor ever seemed more bereft of any say, not to mention sway, in the affairs of state. Gandhi warned of the sidelining of the people by a craze for fancy attractions. His view of journalism makes fascinating reading.*

Ramakrishnan, Niranjan. *Reading Gandhi in the Twenty-First Century*. New York: Palgrave Macmillan, 2013. DOI: 10.1057/9781137325150.

If you were of age some twenty-five years ago, you might still remember the jokes about the old Soviet Union and its official maps of Moscow. Apparently the Soviet government printed nonexistent streets (or left out real ones) in order to confuse the odd American spy (who, no doubt, came equipped with satellite-verified accurate maps anyway).

Information emanating from a deeply paranoid state is transparent in its absurdity. But in an age of market worship, we easily forget that it could be twisted just as much, and far more subtly, by the profit motive.

"If it bleeds, it leads" is the touchstone of commercial television stations everywhere. Television is at its best with visuals, and is well aware of this aphorism. Blood, gore, and sundry catastrophes are too tempting to pass up. But here, too, some grisly scenes are more equal than others. As Lisa Romero writes about a march during the Occupy Wall Street protest:

> I had been one of the hundreds, then thousands, to witness the march from nearly beginning to end—and that was not how I'd expected things to turn out. But, almost on cue (as if to underscore the government's fear this would spread), things escalated quickly and publicly in the glaring view of the Twitterverse, very likely to the chagrin of the NYPD, [New York mayor] Michael Bloomberg and anyone on Wall Street who didn't want this little movement to earn attention or gain credibility.
>
> Within a matter of minutes, thousands of people were logging into the live-streaming site or retweeting the police presence. Yet, the media still weren't covering the event, *except as an aside*, almost.[1] (italics mine)

If, as William Randolph Hearst is reported to have said, "News is something someone doesn't want printed; all else is advertising," what do we make of the non-reporting of or non-perseverance with something happening right at the financial nerve center of the world? What if the media peddled nothing but distraction twenty-four hours a day in the name of news, so that over a few decades people even stopped noticing? To paraphrase the saying "War is too important to leave to the generals," have we left the news too much to the media?

But let us return to the theme of news-as-entertainment, which goes to the heart of the so-called free media. Many books have been written about the consolidation of media control and the increasing cost of setting up any kind of alternative media outlet. Whatever issues the numerous articulate and well-coiffed talking heads might argue over on television, one often finds that their views cover the entire gamut from A

DOI: 10.1057/978-1-137-32516-7

to B. Certain themes and certain viewpoints are taboo. In the "arsenal of democracy," to take just one example, the so-called liberal newspaper of record, the *New York Times*, has not in my recollection published Ralph Nader or Noam Chomsky. I could be wrong, but if so only because their pieces have appeared so infrequently as to not even register.

The story with television is a little more involved. As the late visionary Neil Postman pointed out in his brilliant book *Amusing Ourselves to Death*, TV is inherently unsuited to any serious discussion, a defect made worse by the need to cut to a commercial after half a thought and the easy, all's well that ends well plying of the standard nostrum "We'll have to leave it at that."

None of this absolves the citizenry of its own role in relinquishing its sense. The sad truth captured by Postman's title is no less sad, or true, for its pithiness. The media has treated the population as consumers, and the population has readily slipped into the role. Both have forgotten their duty as watchdogs over threats to the public good and political rights. As cartoonist Ted Rall says, in the United States it has been "40 years of elections without politics."[2]

There is no such thing as a free lunch, nor is there free news. Even the "neutral" Internet search engines have their own biases, and certainly can be influenced by business considerations, as proven by many of them buckling under threats from China. A large part of understanding and grasping the significance of various news items really falls to the citizen. A populace that has "outsourced" this critical task, either mouthing some convenient shibboleth it has been fed, such as "Politics is dirty," or more cynically choosing to go with the stock market index as the measure of societal wellness, is sure to emasculate itself over time. The series of setbacks to the average American over the past three or four decades provides a showcase of how the ascendancy of technology and state-of-the-art media gadgetry can go hand in hand with—or perhaps even result in—the sidelining of the citizenry.

An ancient joke often attributed to the proverbial Sufi wit Mullah Nasruddin has him searching for something under a street lamp on a dark night. A passerby after seeing him thus engaged asks what he is looking for. Nasruddin confides that he has dropped his key. After their joint efforts to find it prove futile, the passerby idly inquires where exactly he might have dropped it. Nasruddin points to a tree dimly visible in the distance. The confused stranger asks why, then, is Nasruddin

DOI: 10.1057/978-1-137-32516-7

looking here, under the lamppost. "Because this is where the light is," explains Nasruddin patiently.

The street lamps of Nasruddin's day are the TiVo, mobile apps, and instant messages of our time, all shiny, bright, and attractive. The mere fact that information is easily available does not mean that it will be accessed, and even if it is, the easier path might well be a decoy to hide some uncomfortable truth. At a time of huge personal credit card debts, the American political class, in full public view, provided giant tax exemptions to the richest in the land while starting two open (and several barely clandestine) wars. If free media was thought to be a bulwark against the country being bamboozled into surrendering its hard-won freedoms, this myth has been exploded over and over in the first decade of the twenty-first century.

The proverbial power of the printed word has nothing on the sway of modern multimedia. A clip on YouTube can push public opinion, or at least distract from several more important things that might be happening, in dimensions a sage columnist with the most closely marshaled arguments can only covet.

In a piece written with an equal measure of sorrow and frustration, the one-time Reagan functionary and erstwhile *Wall Street Journal* associate editor Paul Craig Roberts declared that America was assassinated on September 30, 2011, when two American citizens, Anwar al-Awlaki and Samir Khan, were killed in Yemen on the orders of their government, without any charges, trial, or other due process. The event was briefly noted in the American press, where it was heartily applauded. As Roberts writes:

> The presstitutes and the worshippers of America's First Black President have fallen in line and regurgitated the assertions that Awlaki was a high-level dangerous Al Qaeda terrorist....
>
> But what Awlaki did or might have done is beside the point. The US Constitution requires that even the worst murderer cannot be punished until he is convicted in a court of law. When the American Civil Liberties Union challenged in federal court Obama's assertion that he had the power to order assassinations of American citizens, the Obama Justice (sic) Department argued that Obama's decision to have Americans murdered was an executive power beyond the reach of the judiciary.
>
> In a decision that sealed America's fate, federal district court judge John Bates ignored the Constitution's requirement that no person shall be deprived of life without due process of law and dismissed the case, saying

DOI: 10.1057/978-1-137-32516-7

that it was up to Congress to decide. Obama acted before an appeal could be heard, thus using Judge Bates' acquiescence to establish the power and advance the transformation of the president into a Caesar that began under George W. Bush.[3]

What this bodes for the average American citizen is not even remotely grasped by the very people whose liberties are thus being expropriated. Roberts continues:

> Emotionally, the people have accepted the new powers of the president. If the president can have American citizens assassinated, there is no big deal about torturing them. . . . Instead of seeing the danger, most Americans will merely conclude that the government is getting tough on terrorists, and it will meet with their approval. Smiling with satisfaction over the demise of their enemies, Americans are being led down the garden path to rule by government unrestrained by law and armed with the weapons of the medieval dungeon.

The final check on such usurpations would be a watchful citizenry that can make connections. This would require a high degree of the awareness that seems to have diminished with the advent of the very media purporting to provide exactly that. Fifty years of entertainment as education and TV clips as news seem to have reduced any such capacity in the American population at least. Paradoxically, this fall is best demonstrated by television itself. The late-night comedian Jay Leno has a segment called "Jaywalking," in which he goes out onto the street and interviews random people. These are mainly people in their teens and twenties. A typical question might be "When was the Civil War fought?" or "What country lies to the north of the United States?" or "Which continent is Germany in?" On a good day, perhaps 50 percent of the respondents have the correct answers. Usually it is a lot worse.

Leno will then downshift to simpler questions such as "What is the capital of the United States?" or "Which is greater—one quarter of something or 25 percent?" or "Once in how many years do we have a presidential election?" Even here, right answers are rare.

Assuming that the interviewees are not being facetious or just playing along, I sometimes wonder which aspect of this disaster should appall us more—the abysmal state of general knowledge among so many young people or their complete unabashedness at this fact. The high humor with which they receive the news that they had the wrong century, country, or continent suggests that they are not at all fazed.

DOI: 10.1057/978-1-137-32516-7

Now, one might argue that this sort of "trivia" has been made obsolete by an age in which knowing how to send a tweet is more essential than knowing the number of amendments in the Bill of Rights. But when society can no longer act as if certain things are common knowledge, it can be argued, a whole basis for its stability is undermined. This goes back to what the author E. D. Hirsch referred to as "cultural literacy," the common knowledge that unifies society. Back when I was in graduate school, a professor from a large university came to give a talk, as part of his interview for a chaired professorship in our computer science department. His field, in which he was renowned, was artificial intelligence. Most of his lecture is now a blur in my mind (and was, I'm sure, even then), but one concept remains vivid. As I understood it, his point was that a lot of our knowledge is contextual—information that we know even though it is not explicit.

"Suppose I told you that Henry Kissinger was seven feet tall," this professor began. "You would know I was wrong. How would you know his height? You are unlikely to have seen him. But you would say to yourself, 'If Kissinger were seven feet tall, somehow I should have known about it'!"

The example has remained with me all these years. Upon reflection, it also relates to the politico-cultural awareness of the populace. Just as we all assume some things to be common knowledge, we also assume that some kinds of information will automatically reach us, without any special effort on our part, by what we might call "automatic transmission (of information)," or ATOI.

Many things in modern society depend on ATOI. If a drug is recalled, you expect to learn of it. Same if you have a model of car that is being recalled. If the freeway is shut down, you somehow come to know.

In closed societies, by contrast, genuine information is hard to come by, rumors flourish, and cant and political correctness proliferate, but this does have a "positive" aspect: it leads to a healthy suspicion in the minds of the population as regards the "official story" about anything. The people are constantly on the lookout for any effort by their government to hoodwink them.

Over the years, Americans have begun to believe that, since they are a special people, information will somehow make its way to them with no seeking on their part. This complacency has (and continues to) cost them dearly. Take something as gruesome—and public—as 9/11. Over the past ten years, a number of websites and books have discussed

DOI: 10.1057/978-1-137-32516-7

how what happened on 9/11 cannot be explained by the government's version of events, or the 9/11 Commission's. Arrayed on the other side are a number of equally vehement individuals, many of whom, such as Alexander Cockburn and George Monbiot, are no fans of the Bush administration. These people have nothing but contempt for those they call "conspiracy nuts."

Whatever the truth may be, it is clear enough that the government has still not released a lot of the photographs and other evidence gathered from the Pentagon site. In a larger context, I recall my total surprise on September 12 when the president did not set up a commission of inquiry to find out what had happened. It took a year and a half for the committee to be constituted. Obviously, in any criminal investigation, speed is of the essence. Equally surprising, there was no clamor for such an investigation in Congress or among the public. Certainly there was none from the media, which one would have expected to be vociferous, even strident, in demanding all the details. During the lull, much valuable evidence disappeared. One story I heard was that the metal rubble of the Twin Towers was sold off as scrap to China. Many have raised questions about Attorney General Ashcroft switching to private planes before September 9, 2011, Condoleezza Rice warning the former mayor of San Francisco not to take an aircraft that morning, and the famous "Bin Laden Determined To Strike" memo, although all of these questions are treated with resentment when asked. But better than any specific conspiracy theory is a set of logical, commonsense questions raised by an author known as Werther in a *Couterpunch* article.[4]

My own empirical, unscientific, interactions lead me to think that older Americans would have less difficulty with Jay Leno's questions above than younger Americans. The older generation appears to have a better grasp of the world outside America, of America's own history and, thus, its place in the world. They seem to be less preoccupied with gadgetry, and to have more time to absorb the world.

Reminiscent of the Hitchcock series *Stories My Mother Never Told Me*, news conferences given by the president and other high officials suggest a similar headline: "Questions Our Reporters Never Ask."

An audit of America's downward spiral from a vibrant, industrious, curious, and confident nation full of good cheer to a country beset with so many problems today will find no lack of culprits. None will have left more fingerprints than a rampant media lost in its own fascination with technology while its ever-shrinking cabal of corporate owners

DOI: 10.1057/978-1-137-32516-7

never took their eyes off the prize. As other countries hasten to follow in America's footsteps, confusing free information with corporate-provided information, they might want to take a look at snapshots of the premedia America and its current visage.

Gandhi's answers to distraction and its consequences at both the individual and societal levels can be gleaned from two ideas in his writings. In a letter written to Jawaharlal Nehru in 1945, shortly before Indian independence, he invokes *Hind Swaraj* and reiterates his faith in the basic ideas he had presented in that book nearly forty years previously. Leaving aside the difference in outlook between him and his chosen lieutenant, we can isolate a single sentence that captures Gandhi's canonical approach: "For me, it is material to obtain the real article and the rest will fit into the picture afterwards. If I let go the real thing, all else goes."[5]

In the same letter he says something else of relevance to our current discussion:

> It may be that India too will go that way and like the proverbial moth burn itself eventually in the flame round which it dances more and more furiously. But it is my burden to protect India and through India the entire world from such a doom. The essence of what I have said is that man should rest content with what are his real needs and become self-sufficient. If he does not have this control he cannot save himself.

He was echoing a theme first expressed in *Hind Swaraj*, but repeated several times over the following decades with firmer faith:

> "Civilization, in the real sense of the term, consists not in multiplication but in the deliberate and voluntary restriction of wants. This alone promotes real happiness and contentment, and increases the capacity for service."[6]

Could it be that Gandhi was referring to the calamitous impact modern media often has on national discourse? Not specifically, but he was referring to the general trend of welcoming anything that enhances speed and looks beautiful. Often during the course of his life Gandhi puzzled over the human capacity for megalomania. Men not only tended to acquire more goods than they needed, a weakness that was obvious enough; they also exceeded their wisdom in their solutions (delusions?) of grandeur. Where Gandhi did refer to journalism directly, he wrote:

> I have taken up journalism not for its sake but merely as an aid to what I have conceived to be my mission in life. My mission is to teach by example and precept under severe restraint the use of the matchless weapon of Satyagraha which is a direct corollary of non-violence and truth.... To be

DOI: 10.1057/978-1-137-32516-7

true to my faith, therefore, I may not write in anger or malice. I may not write idly. I may not write merely to excite passion. The reader can have no idea of the restraint I have to exercise from week to week in the choice of topics and my vocabulary. It is a training for me. It enables me to peep into myself and to make discoveries of my weaknesses. Often my vanity dictates a smart expression or my anger a harsh adjective. It is a terrible ordeal but a fine exercise to remove these weeds."[7]

As to any pretensions that an endless desire for cerebral stimulation was somehow superior to corporal urges, Gandhi made no distinction:

> "Therefore the ideal of creating an unlimited number of wants and satisfying them seems to be a delusion and a snare. The satisfaction of one's physical needs, even the intellectual needs of one's narrow self, must meet at a point a dead stop before it degenerates into physical and intellectual voluptuousness."[8]

A culture that has learned to crave endless sensation underwritten by a commercial ethos that teaches never to stop selling may not be receptive to Gandhi's emphasis on self-restraint, either in consumption or in expression. Yet, to paraphrase Bertrand Russell on great lives, great cultures and civilizations may also be unexciting ones for the most part, a sense captured by anti-immigration writer Steve Sailer's tart observation "It's a general rule that the tastier the indigenous cuisine, the lousier the government."[9] It is a straightforward syllogism: where (1) news must make money, and (2) people will watch or listen only if something is entertaining, it follows that (3) news becomes that which thrills, knowledge an obscure factoid about some celebrity, and information advance notice of a discount sale at the mall.

Meanwhile, your country may be drowning in debt and hemorrhaging jobs, while killing hundreds of people in faraway lands whose names you can't pronounce, all in the name of you, the people.

But republics call for informed vigilance. The alternative is virtual reality: pretend issues, faux spats, but real entertainment—well, ratings, anyhow. Unfortunately that *is* the one thing we have gotten rather good at.

# Notes

1    Lisa Romero, "What the Media Aren't Telling You about American Protests," Open Salon blog, September 26, 2011 (http://open.salon.com/blog/lisa_ romero/2011/09/26/what_the_media_arent_telling_you_about_american_

DOI: 10.1057/978-1-137-32516-7

protests). Coverage improved following this article. Also, the protests grew
larger, spread nationwide, and garnered vocal support from several unions.

2    Ted Rall, "America's New Radicals Attack a System That Ignores Them,"
*Common Dreams*, October 3, 2011 (http://www.commondreams.org/
view/2011/10/03–4).

3    Paul Craig Roberts, "The Day America Died," *Counterpunch*, October 4, 2011
(http://www.counterpunch.org/2011/10/04/the-day-america-died/).

4    "Who is Osama? Where did he come from? How did he escape? What about
those anthrax attacks? A half-dozen questions about 9/11 they don't want you
to ask" http://www.counterpunch.org/werther02182006.html.

5    "Letter to Jawaharlal Nehru," October 5, 1945 (http://www.mkgandhi.org/
Selected Letters/Selected Letters1/letter13.htm).

6    *Yervada Mandir*, 1935, p. 16 (http://www.mkgandhi.org/ebks/yeravda.pdf).

7    *Young India*, July 2, 1925; reproduced in *Collected Works of Mahatma Gandhi*,
Vol. 32, p. 78.

8    *Harijan*, August 29, 1936; reproduced in *Collected Works of Mahatma Gandhi*,
Vol. 69, p. 321.

9    Steve Sailer, *Racial Reality and the New Orleans Nightmare*, September 3, 2005.
Available at: http://www.vdare.com/articles/racial-reality-and-the-new-
orleans-nightmare.

DOI: 10.1057/978-1-137-32516-7

# 10

## Technological Titans, Moral Midgets: The Death of Aleksandr Solzhenitsyn

Abstract: *Juxtaposing Aleksandr Solzhenitsyn's death with the opening of the Beijing Olympics establishes a contrast between the simultaneous shrinking of the moral imperative and the arrival of a technological Panglossia. The advance of this combination seems to engender a march toward total monitoring and surveillance, all in the name of "safeguarding freedom."*

Ramakrishnan, Niranjan. *Reading Gandhi in the Twenty-First Century*. New York: Palgrave Macmillan, 2013. DOI: 10.1057/9781137325150.

Somehow it seemed only fitting that Aleksandr Solzhenitsyn should breathe his last just as the celebration of technical wizardry was to reach its crescendo in Beijing; if the twenty-first century has any unifying allegiance, it is to the Diocese of Technology and, indirectly, to its major sponsor, the Church of Globalization. Both command a degree of reverence and blind worship among the elites of the world that is rivaled, if at all, only by the religious fanaticism of *sans-cullotes* up and down the Hindu Kush.

Solzhenitsyn left not a moment too soon. Quite apart from his age, he was a moral misfit in the new world order. He reposed his faith in man and God, not consumer and conglomerate. If men like Arthur Koestler were disillusioned by what befell their brave new world of the 1920s, Solzhenitsyn, to mix metaphors in referring to the Olympics, was destined to win a Triple Crown in heartbreak: disgusted by the Soviet Union, disappointed by the West, and dismayed by what replaced communist rule–a sort of Reign of Dupe and Knave, aka the Gorbachev–Yeltsin *Kleptofest*. An Olympic Games with the theme "One World, One Dream" was an apt coup de grâce for one whose most famous speech was titled "A World Split Apart."

I should begin by confessing to not having read a single one of Solzhenitsyn's books. It was quite by accident some years back that I came across his Harvard speech, and I was struck by its scorching prescience. Delivered in 1978, it could still harpoon the conscience even as the opening ceremonies in Beijing riveted the eye.

If all else is forgotten about Solzhenitsyn, two things will be remembered: first, the fact that he went to jail (a concentration camp, actually) for professing his beliefs, a fate practically unknown among intellectuals in our day; second, his aphoristic message to the Russian people as he was being thrown out of Russia: "Live not by lies." The deadly truth of his words was to become evident to the Soviet Union within a few short years.

Others in our own time, such as Cindy Sheehan and Kathy Kelly, have tried to give a similar message to America, but their words have fallen on equally deaf ears. True, unlike Solzhenitsyn, they and their ilk have not been consigned to some faraway gulag, but what does it say about us and our free press that they don't need to be?[1]

We live in a world of knitted brows, besotted with technology and wedded to fear, hopeful, if not wholly convinced, that the one can negate the other. The few with smiles are those who have known all along that

DOI: 10.1057/978-1-137-32516-7

marrying fear to technology is the philosopher's stone of our times. They are the proverbial ones laughing all the way to the bank.

Naomi Klein has written a fantastic piece on this imminent future in *Rolling Stone* magazine, about how the Beijing Olympics are really the first test case for the technology underlying National Security State 2.0, cameras everywhere with every face photographed and matched in real time.[2] Shorter but entirely brilliant is Fred Reed's one-page essay in the *American Conservative* on the enormous erosion of privacy in our time, and the complete equanimity with which we have countenanced it.[3]

At the Beijing opening ceremony, you saw George W. Bush, who had launched two foreign wars, chatting pleasantly with Vladimir Putin, who had just that day launched his first. Both sat enjoying an Olympics gala whose theme, remember, was "One World, One Dream." Elsewhere the anthrax lie was already being covered up even as it was being exposed, and Edward(s) the Confessor[4] sat for a bare-all interview seeking to mitigate past two-timing with current good timing—to be aired while the world was still being dazzled by the Olympic extravaganza.

"Live not by lies," said Solzhenitsyn. Gandhi would have seconded the statement. In his words:

> If it is possible for the human tongue to give the fullest description of God, I have come to the conclusion that for myself, God is Truth. But two years ago I went a step further and said that Truth is God. You will see the fine distinction between the two statements, viz. That God is Truth and Truth is God.... And I came to that conclusion after a continuous and relentless search after Truth which began nearly fifty years ago. I then found that the nearest approach to Truth was through love. But I also found that love has many meanings in the English language at least.... But I never found a double meaning in connection with truth and even atheists had not demurred to the necessity or power of truth. But in their passion for discovering truth, the atheists have not hesitated to deny the very existence of God—from their own point of view rightly. And it was because of this reasoning that I saw that rather than say that God is Truth, I should say that Truth is God.[5]

Gandhi was being asked questions of a philosophical nature when he gave the answer above, but his insistence on the truth was a fixture in any discussion of political strategy. Whether it was a motley crowd of would-be agitators seeking his guidance regarding the removal of an English colonel's statue or Muslims demanding the restoration of the Caliphate, he made it clear they would get his support provided they did not, in his words, "countenance violence or untruth."

DOI: 10.1057/978-1-137-32516-7

In his autobiography, Gandhi has a chapter titled "The Canker of Untruth," a reference to his deliberately hiding something, even though it was for no malicious purpose. "For experience convinces me," he wrote in a different context, "that permanent good can never be the outcome of untruth and violence," And he added, "Even if my belief is a fond delusion, it will be admitted that it is a fascinating delusion."[6]

As Kamalapati Tripathi writes in his book *Gandhi and Humanity*, Gandhi did not distinguish between violence and untruth. One need not look very far to appreciate that untruth is a form of violence, in the long run more pernicious than actual physical assault. Goebbels relied on it, George Orwell immortalized it in *1984* and *Animal Farm*, modern governments ply it to perfection—the Iraq War being an example of recent vintage.

Living by lies, a practice Solzhenitsyn warned against, is corrosive not only to the soul but to society. Over time its price is steep. Taken in by its half-truths and deceptions, a society no longer able to distinguish between truth and falsehood clings to known lies, fearful of looking for the truth. It descends into an abyss from which no technology can rescue it.

There is an old R. K. Laxman[7] cartoon: The day after an Indian election, when every wall has been plastered with posters several times over, a conscientious party worker returns to scrape them off. The landlord rushes out—not to scold him for sticking posters without permission, but to stop him taking them down. "Don't, don't, don't," he yells anxiously. "Without the posters the building will fall."

Live not by lies? And face the moral choices that would result? Not for us, thanks. *Time* to *Sprint*.

## Notes

1   Niranjan Ramakrishnan, "The Silence of the Lambs," published at the end of the article "Our Own!" *Counterpunch*, February 6–8, 2004 (http://www.counterpunch.org/2004/02/06/our-own/).

2   Naomi Klein, "China's All-Seeing Eye," *Rolling Stone*, May 14, 2008.

3   Fred Reed, "Don't Sweat the TSA," *American Conservative*, May 19, 2008 (http://www.theamericanconservative.com/article/2008/may/19/00035/).

4   John Edwards, former US Senator and contender for the Democratic Party's presidential ticket in 2004 and 2008.

DOI: 10.1057/978-1-137-32516-7

5   Speech at Lausanne, December 8, 1931; reproduced in *Collected Works of Mahatma Gandhi*, Vol. 54, p. 268.

6   *Young India*, December 11, 1924. *Collected Works of Mahatma Gandhi*, Vol. 29, p. 442.

7   A well-known Indian cartoonist, famous for his popular daily "You said it" feature in the *Times of India*.

DOI: 10.1057/978-1-137-32516-7

# 11

# Corruption and Its Discontents

Abstract: *Corruption is a huge problem in many parts of the world. In India it has, of late, received a great deal of attention owing to a self-styled Gandhian called Anna Hazare. The Mahatma himself might have viewed it as somewhat more than a matter of getting the government to pass a new law. Perhaps he would have quoted the Bible: "cast out first the beam out of thine own eye; and then shalt thou see clearly to cast out the mote out of thy brother's eye."*

Ramakrishnan, Niranjan. *Reading Gandhi in the Twenty-First Century*. New York: Palgrave Macmillan, 2013. DOI: 10.1057/9781137325150.

DOI: 10.1057/978-1-137-32516-7

> Hazare *ke Khwaahishen aisi ke har Khwaahish* humdrum *nikale*
> *Bahut nikale unke* demands *lekin phir bhi* dumb *nikale*
>
> (with apologies to Mirza Ghalib)[1]

Judging from the *New York Times* and the *Washington Post*, urban India is abuzz with the idea of banishing corruption. Photographs of peaceful marchers filling a giant overpass have made front-page news. Anna Hazare, whose arrest and fast have ignited the stir in cities all across India and among Indian groups abroad, is now a well-known figure. The fast, meetings, and protests are being billed as nothing less than a second freedom movement.

That last comparison is in perfect pitch with an intelligentsia cut adrift from any sense of proportion, as befits one that until only recently was capable of considering Manmohan Singh a more significant reformer than Mahatma Gandhi.

Amid all the din it is easy to forget the lofty purpose of the "second freedom movement". It is the appointment of an ombudsman and a subsidiary bureaucracy to oversee allegations of corruption among government officials. One might just as soon label a demand for web access to one's income tax records the second Declaration of Independence.

Owing perhaps to his experiences as a lawyer, Gandhi did not view some new law as the panacea for every social, economic, or political problem. He assigned a lot more importance to the renewal of the human being. Gandhi believed that the quality of any country ultimately depends on the quality of its people. His abhorrence of legal cleverness as a means of fixing human problems is best illustrated by E. F. Schumacher in his classic, *Small Is Beautiful*: "Gandhi used to talk disparagingly of 'dreaming of systems so perfect that no-one will need to be good.'"[2]

That corruption is the scourge of daily existence in India as in few other countries may be entirely true. Ordinary people in everyday life have to pay bribes all the way from getting a driver's license to obtaining a housing permit. Certainly many of these bribes are paid to government officials, big and small. The same government officials have to bribe others in their capacity as applicants. Corruption is many things to many people.

Anna Hazare and his acolytes seem to forget—or are loath to admit—that corruption is not limited to the government. They appear to believe that the appointment of eminent Indians to some overseeing council would somehow ensure moral rectitude. If credentials alone, or even a

DOI: 10.1057/978-1-137-32516-7

personal reputation for incorruptibility, were such strong safeguards, the administration of Prime Minister Manmohan Singh should be a case study in civics textbooks on model governance. Instead, it is considered the fount of malpractice and graft on a gargantuan scale, with many reckoning that it presides over the most corrupt dispensation in independent India's history.

Neither the protesters nor the government wants to address the issue of corruption in India in its deeper essence. Is it an obscenity only when a government official receives a bribe? What about corruption of the conscience? For instance, is it corruption when someone can build a sixty-story skyscraper as a personal residence in a country where millions of children go to bed malnourished? Gandhi again: "Every palace that one sees in India is a demonstration, not of her riches, but of the insolence of power that riches give to the few, who owe them to the miserably requited labours of the millions of the paupers of India."[3]

Even though there is a palpable correlation between the size and scope of scams in India and Manmohan Singh's neoliberal initiatives starting in the early 1990s, Anna Hazare and his wise counselors don't seem to want to see it. And amid all the criticism of his ineptitude in dealing with this crisis, practically the first words out of the prime minister's mouth were to caution that it would be wrong to connect corruption with economic liberalization.

As the recently departed veteran journalist Alexander Cockburn was fond of saying, "Never believe anything until it is officially denied."

In 1991, Manmohan Singh, finance minister in a minority government, kicked off a "liberalization" program that laid the foundations for a two-decade neoliberal spree. It has turned some 250 million Indian citizens into celebrated "consumers," but distorted any measure of what Professor Amartya Sen would call "social choice." In this new order, what is good for consumerism and high living is alone good for India, whatever its cost by way of farmer suicides, uprooting of entire villages, pollution of the water table, or handing over of India's agricultural future to the GMO boys at Monsanto and elsewhere. The lone measure of success in this Eastern Wild West is something called the growth rate; the ethos it has spawned would both amaze and gratify Gordon "Greed Is Good" Gecko.

Gandhi's diagnosis and cure for India's corruption epidemic would probably involve a lot more pain and sacrifice than a few genteel marches and TV interviews. He might point out that in a milieu in which leaders

DOI: 10.1057/978-1-137-32516-7

openly promote moneymaking as the most important virtue, and an elite esteems itself according to the extent of its ostentation, corruption could only find a conducive habitat. He would reject recourse to some bill, not for its technical shortcomings, but perhaps because reliance on legislation would "diminish the moral height" of Indians, just as his *khadi* movement urged Indians to boycott foreign cloth and adopt the rougher and costlier homespun, instead of fasting outside the Viceroy's palace and pleading for a ban on English mill imports.

The fervid and often uncivil jousting between "civil society" on the one side and the gentleman prime minister's cabinet on the other, poring over fine points of an anticorruption bill while taking care never to mention the 800-pound gorilla in the middle of the room, reminded me of something I had read long ago:

> One of the greatest of the Bengali novelists of the 20th century, Sarat Chandra Chatterjee, has summed up the underlying principle of Hindu behavior in a neat, if cynical, epigram. He makes a woman who had a low-caste paramour boast that although she lived 20 years with him she had not for a single day allowed him to enter her kitchen.[4]

# Notes

1　*Hazaaron khwahishen aisi ke har khwahish pe dam nikle*
　*Bahut nikle mere armaan, lekin phir bhi kam nikle*
　[Thousands of desires and each a deadly force,
　I have had surfeit of them, still I yearn for more]
　K. C. Kanda, *Mirza Ghalib: Selected Lyrics and Letters*, Sterling Publishers Pvt. Ltd, 28 September 2005.
2　E. F. Schumacher, *Small Is Beautiful: Economics As If People Mattered*, reprint edition, Harper Perennial, 2010, p. 24.
3　*Young India*, April 28, 1927; reproduced in *Collected Works of Mahatma Gandhi*, Vol. 38, p. 323.
4　Nirad C. Chaudhuri, *The Autobiography of an Unknown Indian*, Jaico Books, 1966. p. 418.

DOI: 10.1057/978-1-137-32516-7

# 12

## Of Suicides and Stock Markets:—*Leave It to Psainath*

Abstract: *Indian journalist P. Sainath is famous for his reports about the soaring number of suicides among Indian farmers, a trend that has not abated for more than a decade. The suicides seem to follow directly from policies that have jettisoned every last item of Gandhi's thinking. But many still pretend the deaths are just the result of some odd glitch in carrying out the "infallible" Market Über Alles fundamentalism. Asked by a visiting American clergyman what he most despaired about, Gandhi answered, "The hardheartedness of the educated Indians." Sainath doesn't quote Gandhi. But this chapter does.*

Ramakrishnan, Niranjan. *Reading Gandhi in the Twenty-First Century*. New York: Palgrave Macmillan, 2013.
DOI: 10.1057/9781137325150.

DOI: 10.1057/978-1-137-32516-7

"Only five of the twelve nations affected by the recent [2004] tsunami have a functioning stock market," the speaker began, "and all five markets registered historic or near-historic highs in the week following the tsunami." With that opening, it was impossible not to retain the audience's full attention. Palagummi Sainath, an Indian reporter and writer well-known for his coverage of rural drought and poverty, was speaking at a small college campus, to a crowd of around 200.

Fluent in his subject and familiar (rather too familiar, it appeared at times) with the American lecture circuit, Sainath sprinkled his talk with interesting factoids about the rich–poor divide, the politics of SARS, why he stopped drinking Coke and Pepsi, and a host of other gems. A few examples:

▶ 30,000 homes were destroyed by the tsunami in the town of Nagapattinam in South India. Over 84,000 hutments were forcibly demolished in Mumbai and the occupants evicted, all by the government.

▶ Structural adjustment affects the West too: some 15,000 people died in France in the heat wave in the August of 2003. Their benefits had been cut.

▶ Farmer suicides are not a third-world issue alone: they occur routinely in the United States—only many of them are reported as accidents so that the family does not lose the insurance payment.

▶ Only 1.8 percent of Indian households invest in the stock market, according to the Stock Exchange's apex body, but the finance minister missed the opening day of the new parliament of 2004 because he was in Mumbai to assuage the fears of the market mavens.

▶ Last year, the fastest growing economy in the world was Afghanistan. More than a quarter of its GDP came from opium.

▶ An official body in China concluded that the two fastest-growing segments of the Chinese economy were corruption and prostitution.

▶ India's Human Development Index ranking dropped, during the postliberalization era of "economic resurgence," from 124th in the world to 127th. This put it behind El Salvador, Botswana, and the Occupied Territories of Palestine.

▶ There are now "theme weddings" in India, where a two-acre plot is turned into Hollywood-like set featuring, say, the Taj Mahal. The cost runs to some 30 million rupees ($750,000).

DOI: 10.1057/978-1-137-32516-7

Sainath's talk was entitled "Globalizing Inequality." This title could be interpreted in two ways: one, that inequality was now a global phenomenon, with disparities even in Western societies reaching near Eastern levels, or two, that globalization raises inequalities in local arenas. The talk consisted mainly of examples of the former interpretation. The only references he made to globalization were in passing; one got the impression that he was dismissing any notion of rolling back globalization as pointless, adding mysteriously that the old "think globally, act locally" days were long gone, and we now all need to act and think globally and locally.

Recalling that he had been a history student before becoming a journalist, Sainath described Emperor Nero's open-air party for the *Who's Who* of Rome. As dusk fell, lights were called for, and Nero's staff came up with a novel solution: the party was illuminated by prisoners and poor people being burned on stakes all around the arena.

The thing he had always wondered about, Sainath said, was the attitude of Nero's guests. Why did they go along with this atrocity? How did they continue partying? He ended his talk by asking, "Are we going to be like Nero's guests?"

Brilliant as this was as a rhetorical allusion, the evidence suggests that too many of us have already shown we are willing, even eager, guests. Sainath did not talk about the growing ranks of the middle-class elite in India and elsewhere, determined not to be left out of Nero's party, inuring themselves to the pain of their fellow citizens while simultaneously proclaiming nationalism in every breath, often with genuine belief.

Although the lecture was full of interesting observations, one felt it would have been great if they had been tied together to provide us an insight into why things are the way they are, leaving the audience with inspiration for things to do. Perhaps Sainath felt the facts spoke for themselves.

A couple of post-lecture questions deserve mention. One woman asked about a well-known local dairy cooperative trying to battle Monsanto and resisting the use of a growth hormone in its products. The question: "How can we make sure the big media covers this big story?" It seemed the perfect question, given Sainath's background. The answer was woefully inadequate. After a long-winded reply, much of it irrelevant to the question, all he finally provided were some predictable old chestnuts about writing letters to the editor and the like.

DOI: 10.1057/978-1-137-32516-7

The other memorable question of the evening came from a man who waved about a card he wanted people to sign. It was an appeal to Coke about the Plachimada plant in India. Sainath had referred to this plant in his talk, mentioning how local people were protesting Coca-Cola's deep-drilling, which was draining away the all the ground water in the area. The questioner wanted to know whether such campaigns were useful. Sainath's answer was not noteworthy. It would have been interesting to learn why, when people in Plachimada were being deprived of water because of a Coke plant, so many people in India still continued to drink it. Second, and this was relevant, why did Sainath not once mention the name of the most successful practitioner of such protests in the past century? I mean Mahatma Gandhi. Gandhi would have shamed the country with the moral question of whether it was acceptable to consume a product that deprived people of their drinking water.

Sainath was entirely accessible and easy to talk to. I asked the latter question after the lecture ended. He grew somewhat indignant, first explaining that it was not a prepared speech, then saying that Gandhi was not some kind of deity to be mentioned ritually in every talk. When I persisted, he invoked cloture with a firm "I'm not a Gandhian." I remained unconvinced, for at the heart of all this was the question of how aware people were of what they used, and the consequences of their unconcern. The genius of Gandhi lay in making urban India confront its conscience, and establishing the connection in the urban mind that India could make no viable progress while rural areas were being bled white. I should have liked to know how the methods used in Plachimada compared or to learn of current non-Gandhian innovations.

Right outside was an exhibition of photographs by Sainath of women in rural India. Sainath gave an informal but painstaking tour of the exhibit, recalling how he had come to take each picture and what it represented. He held the small group enthralled with his storytelling, pointing out little things in each photograph that would certainly have escaped the audience otherwise.

Hoping for more of Sainath's insight into the whys of the facts he had cited, I sought permission to join him and his hosts for the remainder of the evening. Why had the political class surrendered so meekly to the onslaught of the phenomenon of "structural adjustment"? He gave an impatient "Everything will be fine, don't you worry" sort of answer: people are fighting; even if some battles are lost, there are still gains. True,

DOI: 10.1057/978-1-137-32516-7

but he didn't address why established bastions of social support systems were collapsing all over the world with little political dissent.

After dinner, we repaired to his host's apartment, where Sainath asked whether we wanted to see photographs of the families of farmers who had committed suicide in Andhra Pradesh. More than 25,000 such deaths had been recorded, Sainath said, "and God knows how many more that have not been recorded." As he laid each photograph on the table, he related the story behind it: who had died, why, the victim's name, his village, his family members, how much he (or she—several women had committed suicide too) had owed, how the family had responded, what they were doing now. It was a numbing rendition. "How do people take their lives?" asked someone hesitantly. "By consuming chemical fertilizer," came the answer. With the seeds gone bad, this was all it was good for. "But why are the seeds bad?" Because the government had silently diluted its standards for seed quality, and then abdicated its responsibility even to impose the watered-down standards. Chalk up one more for structural adjustment.

"But why did these people commit suicide? And why so many?" The loss of hope, the defeat of honor, in most cases. Sainath read out the suicide note of a middle-aged man—a matter-of-fact statement with not a trace of self-pity—saying he had come to his decision because he saw no hope of being able, at his age, to work to pay off his debts and avert dishonor.

Among the suicide photographs was one of a man defeated, a hollowed-out shell of a human being. As we tsk-tsked at that image, Sainath extracted an older photograph of the same man taken a few decades before—alive and virile, holding a tall uncastrated bull on each side, a danger few would dare risk. The later photograph might be a metaphor for the predicament of the political class everywhere: hollowed out.

Just twenty-five years ago, David Stockman wrote a book complaining about *The Triumph of Politics*. A more apt title today might be something along the lines of *The Demise of Politics*. Comprehending and addressing this sea change may be the most crucial component of social activism everywhere.

Sainath is a remarkable journalist, with an incredible memory and eye for detail. He spends more than nine months a year living in the villages. He writes and speaks about poverty and inequity with feeling and sincerity, with great knowledge and understanding. His book *Everybody Loves a Good Drought*[1] has run to 13 editions and several translations.

DOI: 10.1057/978-1-137-32516-7

His articles appear regularly in the Indian press and on the web. The big question is: "Has all this moved our hearts?" Perhaps his next book should be titled *Everybody Loves a Good Book about a Drought.* Sainath himself captured this paradox in his lecture. India has progressed, he said, to the point where a *Dalit (Harijan)* woman can now be elected to Parliament. However, she arrives there at a stage when Parliament itself may be passing into irrelevance. Institutions remain in name, but their intents and purposes have long fled. Hollowed out. We all realize this, but we go on pretending not to notice. As Upton Sinclair said, "It is difficult for a man to understand something when his job depends upon his not understanding it."[2] Gandhi was less gentle in his judgment:

> Come with me to Orissa, to Puri—a holy place and a sanatorium, where you will find soldiers and the Governor's residence during summer months. Within ten miles' radius of Puri, you will see skin and bone. With this very hand I have collected soiled pies[3] from them tied tightly in their rags, and their hands were more paralyzed than mine were at Kolhapur. Talk to them of modern progress. Insult them by taking the name of God before them in vain.
>
> The poor sisters of Orissa have no saris; they are in rags. Yet they have not lost all sense of decency; but, I assure you, we have. We are naked in spite of our clothing and they are clothed in spite of their nakedness.[4]

To paraphrase Gandhi, the farmers who committed suicide had not lost their sense of honor, but, most assuredly, we have.

# Notes

1  P. Sainath, *Everybody Loves a Good Drought: Stories from India's Poorest Districts,* Penguin, 1996.
2  Upton Sinclair, *We, People of America, and How We Ended Poverty,* EPIC Books, 1935, p. 15.
3  A pie was the smallest-denomination coin in British India.
4  From speech at the YMCA, Madras, September 5, 1927; reproduced in *Collected Works of Mahatma Gandhi,* Vol. 40, p. 17.

DOI: 10.1057/978-1-137-32516-7

# 13
# Unbroken Connectivity, Brokered Lives: Industrialism and Its Consequences

Abstract: *"We want industry, let us become industrious,"* said Gandhi. He was referring, of course, to human effort and striving. Modern industry has instead resulted in gigantic human displacements, ecological and environmental devastation, and an alienation of human beings from the very sources from which the food to sustain their bodies comes. Homage to the large machine in the name of efficiency and comfort has, in the end, meant the compromise of our very souls. Gandhi's views on industrialism are among his most prescient.

Ramakrishnan, Niranjan. *Reading Gandhi in the Twenty-First Century.* New York: Palgrave Macmillan, 2013. DOI: 10.1057/9781137325150.

DOI: 10.1057/978-1-137-32516-7

All of modern life, it can be argued, is but an orderly withdrawal from reality: to many children today milk is a chill white liquid that comes out of bottles; eggs are misshapen orbs that arrive in dozens, neatly stacked in gray cartons. We used to laugh at Topsy in *Uncle Tom's Cabin* as she declared she just "growed up." It might be equally funny to reflect that most kids today have scarcely a clue that the plastic-packaged meat in the supermarket really is part of a once live and sentient animal.

Anyway, why single out the children for their innocence, when we see grown men and women, educated and well placed, some even running for president of the United States, proclaim that we are in the Middle East to defend "our oil"; when people who cannot locate Canada on the map clamor to wipe far-off lands from the face of the earth? Odd as it seems, such a disconnect is not only possible; it is pretty much the norm in many aspects of our life.

Unlike primitive cultures, which have festivals calling for serious self-mortification and others involving equally serious merriment, modern climes appear to bring with them a simultaneous attenuation of both sorrow and joy. Kahlil Gibran wrote apprehensively about this trend:

> And the selfsame well from which your laughter rises was oftentimes filled with your tears.
> And how else can it be?
> The deeper that sorrow carves into your being, the more joy you can contain.[1]

Echoing this, the Indian socialist thinker Rammanohar Lohia wrote that modern man was stuck in a routine of joyless comfort. "Comfort" is the operative word of our times; joy a distant concept. In the quest for comfort we have traded away many things inadvertently, over time perhaps even our very souls. Comfort is also the first and last argument for industrialism.

What, if anything, is industrial civilization? It is a lifestyle based on ever-expanding comfort, based on the ability to mass-produce goods (and, in more recent times, services) at one spot and distribute them to faraway places. The other side of the equation is the consumption of goods or services whose making one has no direct knowledge of or connection with.

Since the marginal cost of production is vastly reduced in this model, the larger the market, the greater the marginal profit. From a business point of view, therefore, the quest is to constantly expand markets.

DOI: 10.1057/978-1-137-32516-7

Industrialism dominates our age, with the mass market as the center of any economic endeavor.

We began by tut-tutting at the spectacle of children unable to relate milk with the cow, but that's just the pot calling the kettle black: most of us don't grow or build the things that we eat or use either; really, we don't even know who produces what we consume. The tea and coffee so indispensable to starting our day both take backbreaking effort to plant, nurture, grow, and pick. The spoon with which we stir the sugar (oh, excuse me, the Stevia or Splenda) began its life as a piece of metal ore fetched up from some horrendously hot and perilous hole in the earth that some human being opts to enter every day at enormous personal risk. And at the other end, so to speak, there are other human beings laboring in the city sewers to keep the drainage going. Would you do it, or I? Could we? Why then would someone else? Why *does* that someone else?

Poverty and the threat of starvation are strong motivators, of course. Slavery and risk of physical harm have also served as equally persuasive tools. In some instances, caste and the ideologies related to it have served to seal the deal.

Many decades ago in his book *The Pursuit of Loneliness*, Philip Slater wrote of our attitude to human waste, an inescapable concomitant of being alive. Almost identically to how we deal with the topic of death, we take great pains to put waste out of sight and forget about it. Slater hints at the psychological toll this sort of daily repression entails. But such a dichotomy is hardly new and not limited to this particular disconnect. Even though every record indicates that not one day of his long life did he undertake anything remotely approaching manual toil, the Urdu and Persian poet Ghalib (1797–1869) wrote:

> *ug raha hai dar-o-deewaar se sabzaa Ghalib*
> *ham bayabaan mein hein aur ghar mein bahaar aai hai*
> [Greenery sprouts from the doors and walls, "Ghalib"
> I am in the desert, while spring has arrived home.]

Ghalib's poetry is famous for its obscurity and being open to multiple constructions, but at least one interpretation, not entirely far-fetched, suggests that the poet laments the lack of wholeness, a dissonance between an apparently sumptuous outer life and an inner vacuum, if not despair.

DOI: 10.1057/978-1-137-32516-7

Gandhi, who was born, incidentally, the very year Ghalib died, shared the latter's amusement at the thousand bootless little tangles that led nowhere, the petty worries that occupied the daily lives of his fellow human beings. Ghalib's answer to the futility of it all lay at the bottom of a flask or goblet:

> *Woh cheez jis ke liye hum ko ho bahisht azeez*
> *Siwaaye baadaa-e-gulfaam-e-mushkaboo kya hai?*
> [That for which we hold Paradise dear
> What be it but rose-scented wine made fragrant with musk?]

Gandhi would have rejected Ghalib's solution, not out of a sense of piety but simply because it was incapable of universal adoption, and because it involved an oblique exploitation to boot: for Ghalib to sit all day and write his beautiful verse in homage to the *piyaala* or *koozaa* or *khum* or *suboo* or *jaam*, his genius fired by nightly infusions of rose-scented wine with or without the whiff of musk, others would have to labor in the vineyards, burning under the hot sun.

The lives of these two men who shared initials—Mirza Ghalib and Mahatma Gandhi—missed overlapping by a few months. We can only speculate what Gandhi might have said to Ghalib had they met.[2] But we can get a fair idea from his exchanges with another glorious Indian poet. Though hardly an icon of austerity, Rabindranath Tagore was still far from Ghalib's infatuation with the cup and the flask, although he was open in his skepticism of Gandhi's apparent rejection of the "higher callings" in favor of manual labor.

Tagore sensed in Gandhi's calls to burn foreign cloth and to return to native roots a narrow and atavistic nationalism. A towering intellectual and moral figure even before the Nobel Prize brought formal recognition of his standing, Tagore was held in an esteem approaching worship by the Indian intelligentsia. His doubts were voiced in a highly regarded journal, *Modern Review*.

Gandhi's response, "The Great Sentinel," is a model of respectful but spirited argument. As much as any of his writings, it illustrates the connections he made between industrial civilization, its inherent exploitation of the weak, and the degradation it causes all concerned:

> Our cities are not India. India lives in her seven and a half lakhs of villages, and the cities live upon the villages.... The city people are brokers and commission agents for the big houses of Europe, America and Japan. The cities

DOI: 10.1057/978-1-137-32516-7

have co-operated with the latter in the bleeding process that has gone on for the past two hundred years....

To a people famishing and idle, the only acceptable form in which God can dare appear is work and promise of food as wages. God created man to work for his food, and said that those who ate without work were thieves. Eighty per cent of India are compulsorily thieves half the year. Is it any wonder if India has become one vast prison? Hunger is the argument that is driving India to the spinning wheel....The spinning-wheel is the reviving draught for the millions of our dying countrymen and countrywomen. "Why should I, who have no need to work for food, spin?" may be the question asked. Because I am eating what does not belong to me. I am living on the spoliation of my countrymen. Trace the course of every *pice* that finds its way into your pocket, and you will realize the truth of what I write. Swaraj has no meaning for the millions if they do not know how to employ their enforced idleness.[3]

Mahatma Gandhi's solution to the problem of existence was, so to speak, less fluid than Mirza Ghalib's. Gandhi's prescription was solid physical work. It was work that gave the human being meaning, purpose, and dignity. To find joy and fulfillment in labor was to him the path to liberation. Industry, in its original sense—meaning diligence—was Gandhi's mantra. Well before Gandhi wrote *Hind Swaraj*, an associate had handed him a copy of John Ruskin's *Unto This Last* as casual reading on a long train journey. According to his autobiography, Gandhi was unable to put down the book. All night he read and pondered Ruskin's essays until, by dawn the following day, he had condensed the contents of the book into three ideas:

1   The good of the individual is contained in the good of all.
2   A lawyer's work has the same value as the barber's, inasmuch as all have the same right of earning their livelihood from their work.
3   A life of labor, i.e. the life of the tiller of the soil and the handicraftsman is the life worth living.[4]

As Gandhi wrote later, he had always known and accepted the first idea and vaguely realized the second, but the third idea was a revelation to him. He tried, in vain, to inculcate these tenets in his followers. As columnist Aakar Patel noted, the greatest lesson the Mahatma tried teaching his countrymen was to work with their hands—a lesson that largely fell on deaf ears:

We know that Gandhi borrowed his three great political ideas from the west. He got nonviolence from Tolstoy, civil disobedience from Thoreau and Sarvoday (the rise of all) from Ruskin.

DOI: 10.1057/978-1-137-32516-7

Why these three men? There is something common to them, and to Gandhi's *maru jivan aej mari vani*[5] line. And that is physical self-sufficiency, Gandhi's primary message to Indians: work with your hands.

Tolstoy gave up his possessions, and even his writing, and began a life of labour. In his book *Intellectuals*, Paul Johnson noted that Tolstoy even cobbled his own shoes. Thoreau retreated to Walden and began growing his own food and building a house by himself. In *Unto This Last*, which got Gandhi fired up in South Africa, Ruskin stresses not just the dignity of manual labour, but its equality with all other work.[6]

Ultimately, the roots of Gandhi's suspicion of industrialism lay in his central preoccupation, the liberation of the human being. Gandhi prized the individual's freedom above all else, saying, "The supreme consideration is Man." Outsourcing one's daily needs to others, and soon to unseen hands far away, meant the inevitable rise of dependency and erosion of self-determination. When an American interviewer asked for his response to Henry Ford's proposal to electrify remote villages via transmission wires, making possible "hundreds and thousands of small, neat, smokeless villages, dotted with factories, run by village communities," the rosy scenario failed to cut much ice with Gandhi, who put his finger, as P. G. Wodehouse might say, on the nub of the matter. Gandhi saw right away that none of this would alter the basic issue of freedom:

> while it is true that you will be producing things in innumerable areas, the power will come from one selected centre. That, in the end, I think, would be found to be disastrous. It will place such a limitless power in one human agency that I dread to think of it. The consequence, for instance, of such a control of power would be that I would be dependent on that power for light, water, even air, and so on. That, I think, would be terrible.[7]

Terrible, too, for a less obvious reason, but one that was quite clear to Gandhi, as we shall see. Recourse to out-of-sight providers (human or animal) meant also remaining oblivious to their plight. Witness the growing proliferation of factory farming, representing the industrialization of meat production. Or all the merry talk of towering growth rates even as farmer suicides proceed apace. And this in an age of infinite access to information at light-speed. When asked by a visiting American missionary what he despaired of the most, Gandhi is reported to have replied, "the hardheartedness of educated Indians."[8] The remark is of a

DOI: 10.1057/978-1-137-32516-7

piece with his statement years earlier before an Ahmedabad magistrate, made during what has come to be called "The Great Trial of 1922":

> Little do town dwellers know how the semi-starved masses of India are slowly sinking to lifelessness. Little do they know that their miserable comfort represents the brokerage they get for their work they do for the foreign exploiter, that the profits and the brokerage are sucked from the masses. Little do they realize that the Government established by law in British India is carried on for this exploitation of the masses....I have no doubt whatsoever that both England and the town dweller of India will have to answer, if there is a God above, for this crime against humanity, which is perhaps unequalled in history.[9]

"Little do they know. ... Little do they realize." Gandhi seems to understand that it is not active malice at work here; rather, there is something far more pernicious afoot, the gentle and unwitting cooption of good people, fostered by distance and a conscience made easier with time.

It is precisely such distancing that allows us to lionize twenty-seven-story single-family residences while villages are ravaged by poisoned groundwater. On a global scale, it is the same separation that reduces human killing to a video game played by gleeful youngsters thousands of miles away. When generations are raised ignorant of the roots of their sustenance, dehumanization cannot be far behind.

And in a final act of tragic irony, the separation leads eventually to disenfranchisement of the revelers themselves. The current Occupy movement in America is a revolt by an urbanized population that had all along played the happy consumer, only to wake one day to find it had been undercut in a globalized world whose praises it too was singing until not long ago. That a large number of people still make no connection between the bonanza of cheap foreign-made goods they are enjoying and their own powerlessness—tweeting slogans on cell phones made in Malaysia while protest-marching on shoes sewn in Indonesia—goes to illustrate the mental miasma a hiatus between consumption and production can cause. As James Howard Kunstler noted, well prior to the crash of 2008:

> Among the strange delusions and hallucinations gripping the body politic these days is the idea that the so-called global economy is a permanent fixture of the human condition. The seemingly unanimous embrace of this idea in the power circles of America is a marvelous illustration of the madness of crowds, for nothing could be farther from the truth....
>
> [W]e surrendered the bulk of our manufacturing economy to other nations with cheaper labor and fewer environmental scruples and actually

DOI: 10.1057/978-1-137-32516-7

made the doomed suburban expansion project, and all its ancillary activities such as mortgage-lending, real-estate sales, strip-mall commerce, and easy motoring, the new basis of our economy. This was the dirty secret of our economy from Reagan on: the creation of ever more suburban sprawl and its accessories was mostly what we did in America. Subtract it from everything else and there was little left but haircutting and open-heart surgery.[10]

Thus is freedom lost. No one lands on a foreign shore or crosses a border declaring that they want to rule the country. It always happens over time, and with the uncomprehending or blithe cooperation of the natives. Gandhi, never shy to examine his own faults, taxed his fellow Indians thus:

> The English have not taken India; we have given it to them.... They had not the slightest intention [when they first came] to establish a kingdom. Who assisted the [East India] Company's officers? Who was tempted at the sight of their silver? Who bought their goods? History testifies that we did all this. In order to become rich all at once we welcomed the Company's officers with open arms. If I am in the habit of drinking bhang and a seller thereof sells it to me, am I to blame him or myself? By blaming the seller, shall I be able to avoid the habit? And, if a particular retailer is driven away, will not another take his place?[11]

Similarly might Americans ask themselves after thirty years of a debt-laden spree of luxuriation, Who encouraged illegal immigration? Who wanted cheap goods at any cost? Who promoted outsourcing?"

These are the wages of industrialism vanquishing industry, a prospect that one nondescript little man sitting on a ship on the Atlantic had foreseen, feared, and boldly warned against some hundred years ago:

> [Modern] Civilization seeks to increase bodily comforts and it fails miserably even in doing so.... Formerly, men were made slaves under physical compulsion. Now they are enslaved by temptation of money and of the luxuries that money can buy.... This civilization is such that one has only to be patient and it will be self-destroyed.[12]

Gandhi's words here were echoed almost verbatim, some two decades later, in London by the writer and historian Hilaire Belloc. Summing up a debate he had just finished moderating between George Bernard Shaw and G. K. Chesterton, Belloc concluded:

> This industrial civilization which, thank God, oppresses only the small part of the world in which we are most inextricably bound up, will break down

DOI: 10.1057/978-1-137-32516-7

and therefore end from its monstrous wickedness, folly, ineptitude, leading to a restoration of sane, ordinary human affairs, complicated but based as a whole upon the freedom of the citizens. Or it will break down and lead to nothing but a desert. Or it will lead the mass of men to become contented slaves, with a few rich men controlling them.[13]

# Notes

1    Kahlil Gibran, "On Joy and Sorrow," *The Prophet*, Alfred A. Knopf, 1973.

2    Gandhi not only spoke but wrote a fair hand of Urdu, and it seems impossible that he would not have known at least a few lines of Ghalib. But on the night before he was killed, as he grew somewhat philosophical and, as if in a premonition, even remarked upon the possibility of his being assassinated, it was not Ghalib but Nazir (1732–1830) that he reached for:

*Hai bahaar-e-bagh-e-dunia chand roz*

*Dekh lo tum bhi tamasha chand roz*

[Spring is short in the garden of the world

Enjoy the brave spectacle while it lasts]

This particular verse was part of the Gandhi ashram hymnal (Bhajanavali; see footnote to *Collected Works of Mahatma Gandhi*, Vol. 94, p. 289).

3    *Collected Works of Mahatma Gandhi*, Vol. 24, p. 412.

4    M.K. Gandhi, *Autobiography: The Story of My Experiments with Truth*, BN Publication, 2008. p. 265.

5    "My life is my message."

6    Aakar Patel, "Emotional Lollipop for a Nation of Cretins," *The News*, March 22, 2009.

7    *Collected Works of Mahatma Gandhi*, Vol. 54, p. 22.

8    An anecdote related by Kaka Kalelkar, an associate of Gandhi (http://governancenow.com/news/regular-story/book-gandhi-did-not-write).

9    *Collected Works of Mahatma Gandhi*, Vol. 26, p. 383.

10   James Howard Kunstler, "The End of the Binge," *The American Conservative*, September 12, 2005 (http://www.theamericanconservative.com/article/2005/sep/12/00007/).

11   *Hind Swaraj. Collected Works of Mahatma Gandhi*, Vol. 10, p. 262.

12   *Hind Swaraj. Collected Works of Mahatma Gandhi*, Vol. 10, p. 261.

13   "Do We Agree?"—a debate between G. K. Chesterton and George Bernard Shaw, with Hilaire Belloc in the chair, London, 1928 (transcript at http://www.cse.dmu.ac.uk/~mward/gkc/books/debate.txt).

DOI: 10.1057/978-1-137-32516-7

# 14

# W(h)ither the State?

Abstract: *Be it in China or India, or any other nation, dictatorship or democracy, everywhere the power of the state is in the ascendant. The citizen is a mere cog, trapped in his minor hankerings even as enormous crimes are committed in his name. Gandhi was suspicious of the state, even a benevolent one, for, as he said, it represented concentrated violence. With all the drumbeat of spreading democracy, why has the state not withered away? Why does it instead continue to gather strength, seemingly by the hour?*

Ramakrishnan, Niranjan. *Reading Gandhi in the Twenty-First Century*. New York: Palgrave Macmillan, 2013. DOI: 10.1057/9781137325150.

"In theory," says the wag, "things should be the same in theory and practice. In practice, though, they aren't."

This might serve to explain why every modern state has only grown more powerful over time, instead of becoming irrelevant as theory ordains. Whether a land is ruled by capitalists, communists, Islamists, socialists, or just plain old kleptocrats, and even when it has gone from one ideology to its diametrical opposite, the state itself has never looked discomfited in the slightest degree.

The Soviet state was everywhere. All around was a general fog of great discretion if not blank fear. Everything was bugged. The state had eyes behind every tree and ears beneath every bench. People were afraid of talking to strangers, and picked their words carefully even with friends.

Amid all this was the old joke: a protester was arrested in front of the Kremlin for holding up a sign, "The Politburo is full of idiots." Hauled before a judge, he was given a twenty-five-and-a-half year sentence: six months for disturbing the public peace, twenty-five years for revealing a state secret.

But the greater irony resided in stark fact: the state, which by Marxist theory should by now have been well along its course to withering away, seemed instead to be healthier than ever; a half-century and more of communist rule seemed to have placed it no closer to oblivion than in the heyday of the czar.

But that was Russia with a thousand-year history of tyranny, a Westerner might say. Fast forwarding to twenty-first-century America, we discover a state no less intrusive, if generally more subtle:

> But even Americans who understand the serious consequences of [anti-ter-ror] legislation that diminishes liberties don't always appreciate the extent to which the change in the legal landscape driven by fear of terrorism has also led to a proliferation of mechanisms in the state security apparatus that are being used to diminish the freedoms of each and every American citizen...[1]

The story of security cameras scanning every square yard of London is now old news. The Beijing Olympics as a testing ground for National Security State 2.0, in Naomi Klein's memorable phrase, shows that no state wants to be found lagging in the race to acquire the latest surveillance mechanisms.

The word "state" carries in political science a generally benign connotation, of a dispensation wielding power over a polity. The government of

DOI: 10.1057/978-1-137-32516-7

every country represents a state, but the state itself transcends the parties and individuals currently in power. Speaking broadly, the state represents the permanent interests of a nation. In this essential aspect of the state—being generally accepted as a legitimate possessor of the license to enforce the law, including via the use of force—lies its legitimacy.

Orthodox Marxism would disagree with this definition. Marx derided the classical notion of the state being above party politics and existing mainly to reconcile class antagonisms. To him, the very presence of the state was proof that class struggles had not yet been resolved, the main purpose of the state being for one class to impose its will on another. Only when a classless society came into existence after communism had held sway for some unspecified period—there being no longer any reason for the state to exist—would the state begin to "wither away."

Then there is the suborning of the state to settle private scores. Every time a new government comes into office in some provinces in India, it is not at all unknown for raids to be commenced, arrests to be made, and all manner of cases to be foisted upon political and personal opponents.

With consistent abuse, the state, always a little suspect for its motives, is firmly established in the public mind as just another arm of a particular dispensation, not an impartial and benign entity sitting above the fray. The Hindi adage *Jiski lathi uski bhains* ("He who holds the stick gets the buffalo"), conveys exactly this truth. Conversely, the wielders of state power, too, in such a context, come to view it as a routine accessory to their plans and purposes. That such corruption can seize alike a capitalist, communist, or any other type of state is hardly in question.

Gandhi instinctively grasped the underlying purpose of the state, and therefore its nature; squabbles over its intent to reconcile or suppress class divisions were just a sideshow to a more serious aspect. The state was the antithesis of the individual, and of *ahimsa*:

> The State represents violence in a concentrated and organized form. The individual has a soul, but as the State is a soulless machine, it can never be weaned from violence to which it owes its very existence.... I look upon an increase of the power of the State with the greatest fear, because all the while apparently doing good by minimizing exploitation, it does the greatest harm to mankind by destroying individuality, which lies at the root of all progress.[2]

Nearly three decades after these words, Gandhi's general sense of unease with rampant state power was given more specific voice in an

DOI: 10.1057/978-1-137-32516-7

unlikely quarter, by no less than the leader of the industrialized world. Eisenhower's words of caution could have come right out of one of Gandhi's journals; instead, they were the reflections of a general–statesman as he prepared to retire after two terms as president of the United States:

> [The] conjunction of an immense military establishment and a large arms industry is new in the American experience. The total influence—economic, political, even spiritual—is felt in every city, every State house, every office of the Federal government.
>
> In the councils of government, we must guard against the acquisition of unwarranted influence, whether sought or unsought, by the military industrial complex. The potential for the disastrous rise of misplaced power exists and will persist.[3]

Eisenhower's warnings went unheeded in his own country. In the rest of the world, meanwhile, the military–industrial mindset has taken firm root, not least in Gandhi's own native land, which is plagued by numerous corruption scandals among its multibillion-dollar defense deals. In the five decades since Eisenhower gave his farewell address, spending on weapons worldwide has risen multi-fold. The military–industrial complex thrives.

This would not surprise Gandhi. The modern industrial state to him always appeared a tad specious. While his contemporaries were bowled over by its apparent benevolence and capacity for endless fulfillment of wants, he saw even in its best face a progressive entrapment of humanity with promises of comfort and consequence- (and conscience-) free enjoyment. He saw, too, that modern industry could not be sustained without centralization of power and a commensurate strengthening of the state. Far from being cause for celebration, the rise of a technocracy to mediate between the people and the (industrial) plant often meant citizens ceding sovereignty for creature comforts. To him this was not a step toward human liberation, the instinctive measure by which he reckoned good or bad:

> I suggest that, if India is to evolve along nonviolent lines, it will have to decentralize many things. *Centralization cannot be sustained and defended without adequate force.* Simple homes from which there is nothing to take away require no policing; the palaces of the rich must have strong guards to protect them against dacoity. So must huge factories. Rurally organized India will run less risk of foreign invasion than urbanized India, well equipped with military, naval and air forces.[4]

DOI: 10.1057/978-1-137-32516-7

The endless quest for resources on one side and markets on the other that industrialization demanded, coupled with the military logic required to secure the one or ensure the other, was to Gandhi the road to moral, if not material, bankruptcy:

> The incessant search for material comforts and their multiplication is such an evil, and I make bold to say that the Europeans themselves will have to remodel their outlook, if they are not to perish under the weight of the comforts to which they are becoming slaves. It may be that my reading is wrong, but I know that for India to run after the Golden Fleece is to court certain death.[5]

The wages of pursuing the "Golden Fleece" were seldom better captured than in a piece by the soldier–scholar Andrew Bacevich pondering the shoals upon which a sixty-year spree of consumerism had marooned his country:

> American preoccupation with "more" has affected U.S. relations with the rest of the world. Yet the foreign-policy implications of our self-indulgence are almost entirely negative. Over the past six decades, efforts to satisfy spiraling consumer demand have given birth to a condition of profound dependency. The ethic of self-gratification saddles us with costly commitments abroad that we are increasingly ill-equipped to sustain while confronting us with dangers to which we have no ready response.[6]

In other writings, Bacevich has pointed to the military–industrial state, despairing of the evident incapacity of American democracy to rein in this Frankenstein's monster in either of its incarnations: warmonger abroad or super-secret national security behemoth at home. But Gandhi had anticipated both Eisenhower and Bacevich, getting right to the heart of the matter:

> Science of war leads one to dictatorship pure and simple.
> Science of non-violence can alone lead one to pure democracy.[7]

The thread running through big industry, big arms, and big state is clear enough. To think that a benign and benevolent *chowkidari* (patrolling) was all that would ever emanate from the combination would be to live in a fool's paradise. Nevertheless, Gandhi the pragmatist would be the first to admit that, absent a population capable of innate self-organization and self-restraint, the necessity/inevitability of external control was almost a given. And in the end, what was the state if not

DOI: 10.1057/978-1-137-32516-7

control, congealed, codified, and consented to, one way or another, by the people?

To the former lawyer who preferred bringing about an amicable out-of-court reconciliation between feuding parties to earning more by fighting the case inside, the state could be similarly rendered irrelevant to everyday life by the conscious efforts of the people not to seek its assistance.

It was Gandhi's contention that banishment of "grown-up" supervision, foreign or domestic, must presuppose a maturity among the populace. As Rammanohar Lohia, echoing Gandhi's thinking—if characteristically untainted by Gandhi's notions of restraint in speech and writing—noted famously many years into free India, a country where two people are required to supervise the work of one has nowhere to go but to hell.

It was Gandhi's view that India had lost its freedom owing to the selfishness and greed of its own people; unless they changed and proved themselves worthy of freedom, they would neither deserve nor preserve it. A transfer of power from British to Indian hands would mean nothing without an upshift in consciousness and behavior on the part of both the people and, consequently, the state: "[W]e cannot achieve this political and economic freedom without truth and non-violence, in concrete terms without a living faith in God and hence moral and social elevation."[8]

In an ideal—government of the people, for the people, by the people— world, the state is the populace: "'All land belongs to Gopal, where then is the boundary line? Man is the maker of the line and he can therefore unmake it.' Gopal literally means shepherd; it also means God. In modern language it means the State, i.e., the people."[9] Gandhi makes a deeper point via the Gopal quotation: the state doesn't drop from the heavens but is made by (and of) men and women.

A joke made the rounds on the Internet a few years back. A new entrant to the *paataala loka* (the netherworld in Hindu mythology) notices that there is an American hell, a Russian hell, a Chinese hell, and several others, including, wouldn't you guess it, an Indian hell. While there is practically no activity outside the others, there is a long line to get into the Indian hell. Naturally, the newcomer is curious why, whether the punishment is any different in the Indian hell than in the rest. His guide says, quoting from the tour manual, "All the hells are identical: you have to sleep on a bed of nails, the guy in charge comes and gives you electric shocks every day, et cetera, et cetera." "Why, then, is there such a huge crowd only outside the Indian hell?" the newcomer asks again.

DOI: 10.1057/978-1-137-32516-7

Comes an answer from one of those standing in line: "Here, someone has already stolen all the nails from the beds, the guard is invariably late and frequently absent. More often than not there is no power for the electric shock ..."

So, too, does each state carry echoes of its own population, culture, attitudes, and so on. This mordant remark, attributed to a Russian returning from a foreign trip during the height of the Cold War, says it all: "Amazing, these (East) Germans. They've even made communism work!"

Gandhi would likely have appreciated the joke, for the Indian state he envisioned would be different from others—heck, if an Indian hell was unique, could an Indian utopia be any less so?

> By political independence I do not mean an imitation to the British House of Commons, or the Soviet rule of Russia or the Fascist rule of Italy or the Nazi rule of Germany. They have systems suited to their genius. We must have ours suited to ours. What that can be is more than I can tell. I have described it as Ramarajya i.e., sovereignty of the people based on pure moral authority.[10]

The terms "daddy state" and "nanny state" are often used to describe the stern, authoritarian variety and the soft, welfare-dispensing one, respectively. Their pejorative connotations notwithstanding, both roles are inherent in the state.[11] In the former case, it enforces the law. In the latter, it helps citizens in need. Whether paternalistic or maternalistic, an ideal state, like any good parent, would carry a moral authority that far outweighed its nominal title, and crave nothing more than for its citizens to grow up and throw off the need for "parental" intervention or guidance. The diminution of the state's power depends very much on the nature and maturity of the population.

Maturity would include many things, but ultimately a deep-seated realization of the connection between individual behavior and the public good. In India this would likely always be a huge challenge. Gandhi, in the context of circumscribing state power, could be said to have prescribed two things: self-restraint and trust. Self-restraint implies resisting the temptation to bend or break the law for one's personal benefit. Trust was a tougher proposition in a land where a historically low-trust milieu meant hours of one's day and millions in money spent on policing and litigation instead of living. Not long ago Aakar Patel addressed this point in an article linking culture and corruption: "Why do we have a transactional culture while civilized nations don't? The answer is that we

DOI: 10.1057/978-1-137-32516-7

haven't learnt to trust one another as Europeans have. Indians do not buy the theory that we can all rise if each of us behaves morally, because that is not the message of our faith."[12]

Thus, it was not some stray convulsion of piety that led Gandhi to emphasize the need to trust even the worst opponent. He saw trust as central to a free society. This 1938 exchange with Khan Abdul Ghaffar Khan shows Gandhi alive to a truth only now dawning on many professional sociologists:

> **ABDUL GHAFFAR KHAN:** There are some Pathans in the villages here who persecute Khudai Khidmatgars[13] beyond endurance. They beat them, seize their lands and so on. What are we to do against them?
>
> **GANDHIJI:** We have to meet their high-handedness with patience and forbearance....If we do that it is sure to melt their hearts. If it fails, we shall non-co-operate....We shall brave their wrath but refuse to submit or go against our conscience.
>
> **A. K.:** Would it be permissible for us to lodge a complaint against them before the police and get them punished?
>
> **G.:** A true Khudai Khidmatgar won't go to a law-court. Fighting in a law-court is just like physical fighting. Only, you use force by proxy. To get the police to punish the aggressor is only a form of revenge which a Khudai Khidmatgar must abjure. Let me illustrate my meaning by a personal instance. At Sevagram some Harijans came to me and told me that unless I could get a Harijan included in the C. P.[14] Congress Ministry, they would offer "satyagraha" by staging a hunger-strike....The Police Superintendent wanted to post some police force as he was afraid that the hooligans might do some mischief. But I said "no" to him and told the Harijans that they need not sit outside in the sun; they could occupy any room they liked in the ashram. I offered to feed them too if they wanted. They chose my wife's bathroom. I let them occupy it. We looked after their needs and when one of them fell ill, we nursed him. The result was that they became our friends.[15]

Self-restraint would seem an easier sell in India, where, in Gandhi's day at least, both culture and tradition generally frowned upon personal ostentation while looking up to examples of renunciation and self-abnegation. Nevertheless, there was so much existing disparity that would require enormous passive state violence to maintain or entail a violent overthrow resulting in a brutal dictatorship—unless averted by the wisdom of the wealthy themselves:

> A non-violent system of government is clearly an impossibility so long as the wide gulf between the rich and the hungry millions persists. The

DOI: 10.1057/978-1-137-32516-7

contrast between the palaces of New Delhi and the miserable hovels of the poor labouring class nearby cannot last one day in a free India in which the poor will enjoy the same power as the richest in the land. A violent and bloody revolution is a certainty one day unless there is a voluntary abdication of riches.[16]

Little did the Mahatma know that in just a few decades Indians would show themselves to be world-class consumers, proving to be among the most devout worshippers of big industry, and boasting one of the largest militaries on the planet. Gandhi was clearly off the mark in his estimate of his people's appetites.

But he was entirely on target with his warnings.

Great disparity of wealth persists in India. State violence—and the state's strategic inaction—have both cost untold numbers of lives and livelihoods. The national security complex is alive and well; India, too, has a number of secret government agencies, unanswerable to the public, established in the name of protecting the people (Gandhi didn't even want a CID). Simultaneously, the state has withdrawn from many vital areas of public interest that it alone could safeguard, allowing privateers free rein to work their will, often at enormous loss to the public exchequer, to say nothing of any principles of accountability. Industrialization, privatization, and defense are the new sacred cows, with the growth rate the sole idol to be propitiated, heedless of the price paid in human displacement or environmental hazard. What is true of the Indian state holds true for its counterparts across the world.

What about the people? In the speech referred to earlier, Eisenhower hoped that the American public would keep a keen eye on the burgeoning military–industrial complex so as to keep it from overrunning their very liberties:

We must never let the weight of this combination endanger our liberties or democratic processes....Only an alert and knowledgeable citizenry can compel the proper meshing of the huge industrial and military machinery of defense with our peaceful methods and goals, so that security and liberty may prosper together.[17]

On the fiftieth anniversary of Eisenhower's address, many commentators pointed to his prescience and the unfolding of the very prospect he had feared, some even taking note of the remarkable lassitude with which Americans have tolerated it all. They would not have known that Gandhi had gone one further: keeping the state in line would require not just an

DOI: 10.1057/978-1-137-32516-7

"alert and knowledgeable" citizenry but one actually prepared to offer civil disobedience, always keeping it in reserve as a permanent weapon of good:

> Civil disobedience, therefore, becomes a sacred duty when the State has become lawless, or which is the same thing, corrupt. And a citizen that barters with such a State shares its corruption or lawlessness. It is, therefore, possible to question the wisdom of applying civil disobedience in respect of a particular act or law....But the right itself cannot be allowed to be questioned. It is a birthright that cannot be surrendered without surrender of one's self-respect.[18]

It was Aleksandr Solzhenitsyn who noted that Americans had become legalistic rather than moral. He meant they were lost in interpreting rules and regulations to best advantage. The decades since his Harvard address[19] have proved his words. Bobbing and weaving their way around the statute book in petty pursuit of pecuniary comfort, they have inured themselves to the great heists taking place in their name. The state has been suborned, blackmailed, inveigled, commandeered, and looted in turn as they have fiddled with the latest gadget or gawked at the newest celebrity. Economist and author Paul Craig Roberts is shocked at how placid most Americans have remained in the face of most egregious doings by the state:

> In my lifetime the collapse in respect for, and authority of, the Constitution has been an horrific event. Compare the ho-hum response to the Obama regime's police state announcements with the public anger at President Richard Nixon over his enemies list....Try to imagine President Ronald Reagan announcing that he had a list of Americans marked for assassination without impeachment proceedings beginning forthwith.
>
> Local and state police forces have been militarized not only in their equipment and armament but also in their attitude toward the public. Despite the absence of domestic terror attacks, Homeland Security conducts warrantless searches of cars and trucks on highways and of passengers using public transportation. A uniformed federal service is being trained to systematically violate the constitutional rights of citizens, and citizens are being trained to accept these violations as normal. The young have no memory of being able to board public transportation or use public roadways without intrusive searches or to gather in protest without being brutalized by the police. Liberty is being moved into the realm of myth and legend.[20]

As Gandhi said, civil disobedience is the only—and ultimate—safeguard against a state gone rogue: "it is a birthright that cannot be surrendered without surrender of one's self-respect."[21]

DOI: 10.1057/978-1-137-32516-7

Ay, there's the rub, as the old line goes. For only citizens can have self-respect; consumers merely understand value-for-money. In a silent (no pun intended) metamorphosis, the citizenry of Eisenhower's time has, over the decades, become the consumer society of our own. It is—dare we say it—a transformation devoutly to be grieved. It is also a glimpse into exactly what Gandhi feared a mindless march to industrialism would bring about in India:

> Indeed, the West had had a surfeit of industrialism and exploitation. If they who are suffering from the disease are unable to find a remedy to correct the evils, how shall we, mere novices, be able to avoid them? The fact is that this industrial civilization is a disease because it is *all* evil. Let us not be deceived by catchwords and phrases. I have no quarrel with steamships or telegraphs. They may stay, if they can, without the support of industrialism and all it connotes. They are not an end.... They are in no way indispensable for the permanent welfare of the human race. Now that we know the use of steam and electricity, we should be able to use them on due occasion and after we have learnt to avoid industrialism. Our concern is, therefore, to destroy industrialism at any cost.
>
> India has lived till now when other nations have perished because "she has adapted herself to changing conditions." Adaptability is not imitation. It means power of resistance and assimilation. India has withstood the onslaughts of other civilizations because she has stood firm on her own ground. Not that she has not made changes. But the changes she has made have promoted her growth. To change to industrialism is to court disaster.[22]

## Notes

1 Philip Giraldi, "Big Brother Has Arrived" (http://original.antiwar.com/giraldi/2011/08/10/big-brother-has-arrived/).
2 Gandhi's "Interview with NK Bose," 1934; reproduced in *Collected Works of Mahatma Gandhi*, Vol. 65, p. 318.
3 Eisenhower's farewell address, 1961 (http://avalon.law.yale.edu/20th_century/eisenhower001.asp).
4 *Harijan*, December 30, 1939; reproduced in *Collected Works of Mahatma Gandhi*, Vol. 77, p. 165 (italics mine).
5 *Young India*, April 30, 1931; reproduced in *Collected Works of Mahatma Gandhi*, Vol. 52, p. 9.
6 Andrew Bacevich, "Appetite for Destruction", *The American Conservative*, September 8, 2008.

DOI: 10.1057/978-1-137-32516-7

7    "If I Were a Czech", *Harijan*, October 15, 1938; reproduced in *Collected Works of Mahatma Gandhi*, Vol. 74, p. 89.

8    Speech at Exhibition Ground, Faizpor, December 27, 1936; published in *Harijan*, January 2, 1937; reproduced in *Collected Works of Mahatma Gandhi*, Vol. 70, p. 232.

9    Ibid., pp. 232–233.

10   Ibid., p. 232.

11   The Raj was actually called *Mai-baap* (literally "mother–father") in the Indian countryside.

12   Aakar Patel, "Our Gold-Plated Culture of Corruption," *LiveMint*, April 28, 2011 (http://www.livemint.com/articles/2011/04/28195842/Our-goldplated-culture-of-cor.html).

13   A nonviolent volunteer force in the NWFP (today's Khyber Pakhtunkhwa province in Pakistan) raised by Khan Abdul Ghaffar Khan.

14   Central Provinces, currently part of the Indian state of Madhya Pradesh.

15   "Talk with Abdul Ghaffar Khan", On or before October 15, 1938. *Collected Works of Mahatma Gandhi*, Vol. 74, p.106–107.

16   "Constructive Programme: Its Meaning and Place," *Collected Works of Mahatma Gandhi*, Vol. 81, p. 366.

17   Eisenhower's farewell address, 1961 (http://avalon.law.yale.edu/20th_century/eisenhower001.asp).

18   *Young India*, January 5, 1922; reproduced in *Collected Works of Mahatma Gandhi*, Vol. 22, p. 392.

19   See Chapter 10.

20   Paul Craig Roberts, "The Outlook for the New Year," January 3, 2012. http://www.informationclearinghouse.info/article30151.htm (http://www.paulcraigroberts.org).

21   "The Immediate Issue", *Young India*, January 5, 1922. *Collected Works of Mahatma Gandhi*, Vol. 25, p.392.

22   *Collected Works of Mahatma Gandhi*, Vol. 36, p. 382.

DOI: 10.1057/978-1-137-32516-7

# Epilogue: Where Do We Go from Here?

> All perfectly true, no doubt; but not the sort of thing
> to spring on a lad with a morning head.
> (P. G. Wodehouse, *Carry On, Jeeves*)

Many years ago I used to work for a bank, at its main branch in a small city in Central India. I was a new recruit fresh out of training in the North, and this was my first posting. The manager of the branch was an elderly gentleman from South India, an orthodox Brahmin who wore a red vertical stripe on his forehead. He had spent his entire career in the South until some malicious functionary in head office, doubtless possessed of a twisted sense of humor, decided that he should spend the last months of his career presiding over a branch in a region whose language he did not speak and whose ways he could never fathom. The unruliness and general turmoil he encountered in this practically alien landscape were completely different from anything he had witnessed previously during his long and placid tenure in his own state.[1]

His strategy in response to this torment was simple. He would just wait out the calendar, minimally involving himself in office matters as he stayed bolted up in his cabin and marked his days until retirement.

Ramakrishnan, Niranjan. *Reading Gandhi in the Twenty-First Century*. New York: Palgrave Macmillan, 2013. DOI: 10.1057/9781137325150.

Nonetheless, as he was chief of the place, it was inevitable that some problems would eventually find their way to his office. On such occasions, after listening patiently to all sides, with a pained expression and piteous look that seemed to cry out "Why can't you leave me alone?," he would shake his head sadly as he issued his verdict: "At this rate, branches in the South are a hundred times better." The various contending parties clamoring for a directive would all be equally dumbstruck at this copybook *non sequitur*, but there was nothing more to be got out of the old gentleman. After a while they would all troop out, and matters would chug along, as firmly unresolved as before.

A writer commending Gandhi's words to the twenty-first century runs the risk of sounding rather like my old branch manager, offering little more than a vague wistfulness, giving the reader an entirely wrong impression of Gandhi's message and method, for Gandhi was anything but wistful and seldom helpless.

Nevertheless, looking around us there is certainly plenty to argue that Gandhi may be out of date, even out of place, in our current context. A world infinitely more complicated, connected, and conflicted than in Gandhi's time hardly seems the venue to advance his prescriptions of smallness, localness, and self-restraint. Before talking about where we go from here, therefore, it is fair that we examine some key elements of the "Gandhi is *passé*" meme.

## Technology is not going away

There exists a large and legitimate body of opinion that counts science and technology as the key to the future—indeed, a brighter and better future. Its members and spokespeople comprise practically a *Who's Who* of the world's leaders, and come from every field. The developments of recent decades, such as the revolutionizing of computer networks and media and the sea change they have engendered in how the world goes about its business, all point them in this direction.

## Consumption culture is unlikely to reverse

Even if there were something to say for simple living and restraint on one's appetites, is a world that has now glimpsed the cushy ways of the West—through the proliferation of media and connectivity noted above—likely to settle for anything but the highest living standards, notwithstanding the concomitant load on the environment? So goes one

DOI: 10.1057/978-1-137-32516-7

argument. Another proposition is more strident still. With passionate advocates such as Thomas Friedman at its head, it contends that the consumption urge is like a natural force, and that if only we take advantage of its positive potential, including its "civilizing" effects (such as the Arab Spring), we would be well on our way to a global renaissance.

## Globalism will roll on

There cannot be a globalization without galloping consumption. The loss of jobs in traditional sectors this may entail, whether in America or in the third world, is regrettable but inevitable, just like the vanishing of all the ancillary industries associated with the old horse and buggy (which is frequently trotted out as an example). What the US military has come to term "collateral damage" is roughly how the advocates of globalism in every country view the pain and suffering that might stem from treating the world as one profit center: a bit of dislocation and dysfunction for a large and worthy cause.

## Combining religion and *la dolce vita* is now normal

God knows there is no dearth of religious following in the world. Here, too, despite the old teaching of every creed—from Christianity's "poverty of Christ" to Prophet Mohammad's "my poverty is my pride" to the mendicant traditions of Hinduism, Buddhism, and Jainism—we have gravitated toward mega-churches with millionaire preachers and Saffron-clad gurus in Mercedes Benzs. The old linkage between spiritual advancement and limitation of material wants has been speedily obliterated, until the so-called spiritual leader seems indistinguishable from the sundry car salesman on the make. In this context, religiosity has become completely compatible with greed, rapacity, and endless consumption. An entire basis for either the inward quest or ethical living has been scooped out from the average consciousness.

## "Public bad, private good" is now common wisdom

Bertrand Russell may have coined the phrase "private excellence and public good" to capture the ideal life's pursuit, but in our day we have become far more accustomed to the notion of private profit and public loss. The idea that government is untrustworthy (when it is not evil incarnate) has taken root in many constituencies. Alongside has gained

DOI: 10.1057/978-1-137-32516-7

ground a subordinate but even more powerful precept: that every activity is to be measured mainly in terms of efficiency and profit. As a result, one often finds oneself seriously having to make the case that there are functions for which the return on investment is realized not in dollars and cents or on quarterly balance sheets, but in the long-term stability and sustainability of society itself. Nevertheless, any vision that does not include immediate and substantial moneymaking at its heart may have a difficult time finding purchase.

## Militarism is now so prevalent that it is no longer noticed

Perhaps nowhere should the hollowness of modern civilization appear more starkly evident than in its continuing legacy of death and devastation. Writing in 1951, Albert Camus noted, "One might think that a period which, in a space of fifty years, uproots, enslaves, or kills seventy million human beings should be condemned out of hand."[2] Camus was still totting up numbers from a time before Chairman Mao's several bloody excursions into social reengineering, a decade prior to America's Vietnam War, and ahead of the numerous proxy conflicts of the Cold War and the genocides in Cambodia, East Timor, and Rwanda, not to mention the killings in Afghanistan and Iraq in the current century. We continue to listen and nod our heads as leaders of the world speak well and easily of new world orders, even while they dispatch ever-more soldiers and missiles, all in the name of promoting peace. The tale of the Emperor's new clothes is reenacted before the eyes of the world each day, and carried without a trace of irony on the front pages of the newspapers. Disarmament is a dud.

## With the proliferation of media, everyone believes that information is free

With everybody in possession of a television, a smart phone, and an Internet connection twenty-four/seven, how can one be ignorant of the news? Equally, with so many avenues of entertainment, is it even possible any longer to get anyone's attention for any serious discourse or decisions? Like Edgar Allen Poe's purloined letter, it is easy to miss vital information amid the cacophony of video clips, celebrity tidbits, and general noise. The most difficult aspect of all is the conviction that we are well informed just because we have the technology to be so. What constitutes news is itself a separate question. Most people judge the relative importance of various news items by the font size in which they

DOI: 10.1057/978-1-137-32516-7

are printed or the order in which they are featured on a TV program. In a climate where people have been conditioned to receive entertainment and excitement practically every waking moment, who would listen to a man suggesting calm, simplicity, and contemplation?

## Individual liberties are negotiable in exchange for comfort and safety

The erosion of individual liberties, from a relentless growth of technological capabilities on the one hand and the rise of terrorist threats and fears on the other, it is argued, is only natural. It is a compromise that is universally accepted in practice even if it is decried with great earnestness in living rooms.

## Civil disobedience worked in the old days; it will not work now

As far as Gandhi's methods of political action are concerned, these too have fallen into some disrepute, partly owing to their cavalier use, misuse, or abuse by lesser beings, but also because they appear inadequate in the face of the many new situations confronting the modern age. There is genuine questioning of how a Gandhi might have fared against an Al-Qaeda or a Taliban. Moreover, can there be a Gandhian movement without a Gandhi, or at least a Martin Luther King or someone of suitable moral stature?

## Corruption and the environment are two areas of lingering doubt

In two areas alone does there seem to be some sense of doubt. One is the growth of corruption, both in size and scope. The other is the degradation of the environment, the references to melting ice and rising water levels being the most evident manifestation of this angst. The first is often explained away as a third world phenomenon, with hopes expressed that suitable regulations and cultural recalibrations will provide a suitable corrective. In the matter of the environment, media-led campaigns such as "Reduce, Reuse, Recycle," along with technological advances such as resorting to nuclear power, are expected to do the same. Meanwhile, ethnic, religious, sectarian, and—depending on whom you ask, civilizational—rifts continue to vex every region and continent. Here, too, the

DOI: 10.1057/978-1-137-32516-7

usual nostrum is more economic progress. The urban sprawl continues unabated in every nation, a sign of a healthy growth rate.

By way of summarizing these arguments against taking Gandhi seriously in our time, we may class those making them into two groups. The optimist sees Gandhi as outmoded, if not just plain wrong. It's a wonderful world, humming with innovation and technological breakthroughs, where every country is on its way to becoming an America. The pessimist, while conceding all of the problems attending the optimist's vision, feels it unrealistic to expect a modern population with a hugely attenuated attention span to pay any regard to Gandhi or anyone else suggesting that it radically change its ways.

Somewhere in between these two categories are people such as Bertrand Russell. While sympathetic to many of Gandhi's stances and admiring of him for his bravery and moral sense, Russell thought the nation whose destiny Gandhi had shaped for a third of a century must now leave him behind as it hurried into modernity:

> For India, which is not a modern country, his character and his religion were what was needed. A more modern-minded man, for example, could not have been nearly so successful in the campaign on behalf of the untouchables. But while his memory deserves to be revered, it would be a mistake to hope that India will continue to have the outlook that to him seemed best. India, like other nations, has to find her place in the modern world, not in the dreams of a bygone age. His work is done and if India is to prosper, it must be along other roads than his.[3]

For its part India appears to have taken this counsel entirely to heart, promptly jettisoning Gandhi per his lordship's advice. India is today a poster child for a brave new world where we are allowed to question everything except the mantras of development and growth. To do so is to risk tilting at modernity, a career-limiting move at the very least. It was one of Gandhi's great strengths, fortunately, that he never cared whether he appeared modern or traditional. He saw a false modernity based upon greed, large-scale exploitation, and endless selling for exactly what it was: a giant Ponzi scheme that would leave the world in a moral, economic, and environmental shambles. He hoped to save India, and by its example the world, from what he saw as a straight line to disaster:

> I must not fear if the world today is going the wrong way. It may be that India too will go that way and like the proverbial moth burn itself eventually

DOI: 10.1057/978-1-137-32516-7

in the flame round which it dances more and more furiously. But it is my burden to protect India and through India the entire world from such a doom.[4]

It is not necessary to pit Gandhi's arguments against every single technological advance or scientific innovation, any more than we need to test Newton's laws for every new material or shape. For Gandhi, it was in the end an eternal and persistent question: "How does one live ethically?" No technology can alter the fact of life, birth, and death. Until one faces up to this fundamental issue of human existence, everything else is a mirage. Distinct from most politicians, he disdained the promise of endless material gratification. More fundamentally, he had grasped early in life that there could be no technological answers to essentially moral questions, a notion he reiterated often: "The evil does not lie in the use of bullock-carts. It lies in our selfishness and want of consideration for our neighbours. If we have no love for our neighbours, no change, however revolutionary, can do us any good."[5]

Thinkers as diverse as Mark Twain, George Bernard Shaw, and Karl Marx saw it differently. They felt that material prosperity was the road to a better morality. To Gandhi, a society without moral instincts, self-restraint, or any ethics beyond what can be legally proved was bound to self-destruct no matter what its outward material wealth or military strength. The riots of 2011 in the United Kingdom and the widespread desperation in the former Soviet Union are but illustrations of Gandhi's thesis. To Gandhi, India provided hope because it was still, at least in his time, anchored in some sense of self-abnegation and voluntary self-restraint. Like Vivekananda before him, Gandhi felt that there was still something glorious about a poor country where the most indigent and unlettered individual was nevertheless philosophical. He was echoing a pervasive Indian outlook on life when he wrote:

> Hinduism, Islam, Zoroastrianism, Christianity and all other religions teach that we should remain passive about worldly pursuits ..., that we should set a limit to our worldly ambitions and that our religious ambition should be illimitable. Our activity should be directed into the latter channel.[6]

Gandhi was not apologetic about his conclusion that the solution to problems caused by human greed could not be more greed. Ultimately, the path lay in the limitation of wants, not their expansion. Whether this is a proposition that can be advanced to a world increasingly in thrall to advertisers and marketers using every avenue and every minute to make a

DOI: 10.1057/978-1-137-32516-7

sale is certainly open to question. Ralph Nader has written movingly about the cynicism with which advertisers target even toddlers. One would think there would be widespread outrage against such practices, but we live in a quiescent age. None of this makes Gandhi's proposition any less true.

It is a paradox of our times that with the availability of the finest gadgetry and every form of material sustenance, the individual has seldom been more powerless or redundant. Gandhi's perception has been proven right, in that the more a human being is regarded as an economic entity, the less he remains an individual.

The world, according to his view, was made up of individuals, and disfiguration of this structure could not but result in a distortion of the aggregate. Toward the end of his life, writing to his associate and heir, Jawaharlal Nehru, he says that "man should rest content with what are his real needs and become self-sufficient. If he does not have this control he cannot save himself. After all the world is made up of individuals just as it is the drops that constitute the ocean. This is a well-known truth."[7]

All the arguments listed earlier questioning the practicability of Gandhi's ideas are true in a limited sense, some of them even obvious. The "obvious" is inertia's customary resort against the trouble of changing for the wiser. I use the word "obvious," too, because Gandhi can be classed with Galileo or even Einstein in the way he kept on challenging the conventional wisdom. As anyone originating a new paradigm must seem, Gandhi often appeared to be unrealistic, if not unreal. A man leading a population of 300 million facing a foreign ruler of infinitesimally smaller numbers declared that he would rather go without his country's freedom than have it won by violent or deceitful means. A man who had guided his ancient land of freedom in a manner unprecedented in history chose to observe the day of independence not by whooping it up in the capital city, but by fasting half way across the continent to bring peace among rioting factions. A man whose intelligence and business acumen could have made him a top industrialist saw instead the depredation set in motion by industrialism and spoke out against it. There was nothing conventional about Gandhi, and the fundamental questions he raised will not be wished away by conventional wisdom.

A strange but striking tribute, though it never mentions Gandhi, appears in a recent article by Morris Berman. Called "The Waning of the Modern Ages," it declares that the modern age and all that it connotes are at a dead end, and that what is called for is nothing short of a new "Civilizational Paradigm." Berman might have added that one of the

DOI: 10.1057/978-1-137-32516-7

chapters in *Hind Swaraj* is titled "What Is True Civilization?" The book was written in 1909. That the question was still exercising Gandhi twenty years later is evident from a quip attributed to him during his visit to England in 1931: asked by a reporter, "Mr. Gandhi, what do you think of modern civilization?" he is said to have replied, "I think it would be a good idea."

Albert Einstein propounded the General Theory of Relativity in 1915. It wasn't until 1919 that it was actually verified. Gandhi declared modern civilization unsustainable back in 1909. He was not making this argument because he was familiar with global warming, housing bubbles, or collateralized debt obligations. Instead, it was because he saw the Emperor's new clothes for what they were. Modern civilization based on heavy industry and centralization required an ongoing bubble of consumers. It was debasing to all concerned, and life-destroying to millions. As Einstein's theory was proved experimentally four years later at Principe, a century later we can see every element of Gandhi's warnings coming true in fear-stricken populations and rudderless leaders trading away every vestige of human dignity for promises of safety and economic welfare. "We pretend to work and they pretend to pay us" went the old Soviet-era joke. "We have met the enemy, and he is us," as Walt Kelly said.

Morris Berman notes in his article:

> [V]ested interests, in both the economic and psychological sense, have every reason to maintain the status quo. And as I said, so does the man or woman in the street. What would our lives be without shopping, without the latest technological toy? Pretty empty, at least in the U.S. How awful, that capitalism has reduced human beings to this.[8]

This is exactly the erosion Gandhi had foreseen and warned against. In Gandhi's view, this was one end result of an alienation from one's sources of sustenance. "Outsourcing" the basics of one's daily living would eventually lead to the loss of human dignity, to his mind the greatest tragedy imaginable.

But would a population busy figuring out the latest neat feature in one gadget when it wasn't trying to get the best deal on the next have any patience with someone telling it to toss the whole darn thing into the ocean, as Gandhi once persuaded his associate Hermann Kallenbach to do with his expensive pair of binoculars?

The answer to "Where do we go from here?" lies in whether we are willing to abandon the conditioning of "a new excitement every minute"

DOI: 10.1057/978-1-137-32516-7

and pay attention to the nature of our own lives and of our surroundings. Gandhi had thought a great deal about the corrosive effect of constant thrill. "There is more to life than increasing its speed" is a quip often attributed to him. But he wrote at greater length about the essential nature of the mundane:

> All natural and necessary work is easy. Only it requires constant practice to become perfect, and it needs plodding. Ability to plod is Swaraj. It is yoga. Nor need the reader be frightened of the monotony. Monotony is the law of nature. Look at the monotonous manner in which the sun rises. And imagine the catastrophe that would befall the universe, if the sun became capricious and went in for a variety of pastime. But there is a monotony that sustains and a monotony that kills. The monotony of necessary occupations is exhilarating and life-giving. An artist never tires of his art. A spinner who has mastered the art, will certainly be able to do sustained work without fatigue. There is music about the spindle, which the practiced spinner catches without fail. And when India has monotonously worked away at turning out Swaraj, she will have produced a thing of beauty, which will be a joy forever.[9]

Would anyone today listen? Gandhi himself would not have been too bothered:

> The message [of the Buddha] is 2,500 years old, but it has not yet been truly lived. But what are 2,500 years? They are but a speck in the cycle of time. The full flower of non-violence which seems to be withering has yet to come to full bloom.[10]

Moreover, as a practical politician he was quite modest about his power over a recalcitrant populace, even during his own lifetime:

> You will see that my influence, great as it may appear to outsiders, is strictly limited. I may have considerable influence to conduct a campaign for redress of popular grievances because people are ready and need a helper. But, I have no influence to direct people's energy in a channel in which they have no interest.[11]

The reader has by now perhaps gathered that the author is favorably disposed toward Gandhi's sayings and writings. In this last instance, though, I somehow prefer Jawaharlal Nehru's assessment over the Mahatma's own, made in a speech shortly following Gandhi's assassination:

> the light that shone in this country was no ordinary light. The light that has illumined this country for these many years will illumine this country

DOI: 10.1057/978-1-137-32516-7

for many more years, and a thousand years later that light will still be seen in this country, and the world will see it and it will give solace to innumerable hearts. For that light represented the living truth…the eternal truths, reminding us of the right path, drawing us from error, taking this ancient country to freedom.[12]

If this book has in any measure been able to draw aside the innumerable twenty-first-century *purdahs* of distraction and obfuscation to let in the clear sunshine of Gandhi's intellect and foresight, it will to that extent have been a success.

# Notes

1   I forbore from telling him that things were much wilder in branches further North, where I had spent my year of training.
2   Albert Camus, *The Rebel*, Penguin Modern Classics, 1972.
3   Bertrand Russell, "Mahatma Gandhi," *Atlantic Monthly*, Vol. 190, No. 6, December 1952 (http://www.mkgandhi.org/articles/russel.htm).
4   Letter to Jawaharlal Nehru, October 5, 1945; reproduced in *Collected Works of Mahatma Gandhi*, Vol. 88, p. 119.
5   *Young India*, October 7, 1926; reproduced in *Collected Works of Mahatma Gandhi*, Vol. 36, p. 382.
6   *Hind Swaraj. Young India*, October 7, 1926; reproduced in *Collected Works of Mahatma Gandhi*, Vol. 36, p. 382.
7   Letter to Jawaharlal Nehru, October 5, 1945 (http://www.gandhi-manibhavan. org/gandhicomesalive/comesalive_letter29.htm).
8   Morris Berman, "The Waning of the Modern Ages," *Counterpunch*, September 20, 2012 (http://www.counterpunch.org/2012/09/20/the-waning-of-the-modern-ages/).
9   "A Confession of Error," *Young India*, August 18, 1921; reproduced in *Collected Works of Mahatma Gandhi*, Vol. 24, p. 111
10  *Harijan*, December 24, 1938; reproduced in *Collected Works of Mahatma Gandhi*, Vol. 74, p. 295
11  Interview with foreign correspondents, July 15, 1942; reproduced in *Collected Works of Mahatma Gandhi*, Vol. 83, p. 105.
12  *Selected Works of Jawaharlal Nehru* ,Vol. 5, p. 35. Jawaharlal Nehru Memorial Fund, 1988.

DOI: 10.1057/978-1-137-32516-7

# Bibliography

Joe Bageant (2007), *Deer Hunting with Jesus–Dispatches from America's Class War*, Crown.

Bhabani Bhattacharya (1969) *Gandhi, the Writer: The Image as it Grew*, National Book Trust, India.

Albert Camus (1972) *The Rebel*, Penguin Modern Classics.

Nirad C. Chaudhuri (1994) *The Autobiography of an Unknown Indian*, Jaico Books.

Jared Diamond (1999) *Guns, Germs, and Steel: The Fates of Human Societies*, WW Norton & Co.

Louis Fischer (2002) The Essential Gandhi: *An Anthology of His Writings on His Life, Work, and Idea*,Vintage.

M. K. Gandhi (1933) *Speeches and Writings of Mahatma Gandhi*, 4th edition, G. A. Natesan & Co.,Madras

M. K. Gandhi (1999) *Collected Works of Mahatma Gandhi*, 98 volumes, Publications Division, Government of India.

M. K. Gandhi (2008) *Autobiography: The Story of My Experiments with Truth*, BN Publication.

Kahlil Gibran (September 1, 1973) *The Prophet*, Alfred A. Knopf.

E.D. Hirsch, Jr. (1988) *Cultural Literacy: What Every American Needs to Know*, Vintage Books.

Eric Hofer (1996) *The Temper of Our Times*, Buccaneer Books.

Samuel P. Huntington (August 2, 2011) *The Clash of Civilizations and the Remaking of World Order*, Updated edition, Simon & Schuster.

DOI: 10.1057/978-1-137-32516-7

Uma Iyengar and Lalitha Zachariah (2011) *Together They Fought: Gandhi-Nehru Correspondence: 1921-1948*, Oxford.

Kaka Kalelkar (1960) *Stray Glimpses of Bapu*, 2nd edition, Navajivan Publishing House.

KC Kanda (2005) *Mirza Ghalib: Selected Lyrics and Letters*, Sterling Publishers Pvt. Ltd.

Naomi Klein (October 24, 2008) *The Shock Doctrine*, Picador.

David Landes (1999) *The Wealth and Poverty of Nations: Why Some Are So Rich and Some So Poor*, WW Norton & Co.

Rammanohar Lohia (1963) *Marx, Gandhi and Socialism*, Navhind.

Daniel Patrick Moynihan (February 25, 1993) *Pandaemonium: Ethnicity in International Politics*, First Edition edition, Oxford University Press, USA.

Neil Postman (2005) *Amusing Ourselves to Death: Public Discourse in the Age of Show Business*, Penguin Books.

P. Sainath (1996) *Everybody Loves a Good Drought: Stories from India's Poorest Districts*, Penguin Books.

V.D. Savarkar (1969) *Hindutva; Who is a Hindu?*, Veer Savarkar Prakashan.

E.F. Schumacher (2010) *Small Is Beautiful: Economics as if People Mattered*, Reprint edition (October 19, 2010), Harper Perennial.

Shrilal Shukla (1992) *Raag Darbari*, Translated by Gillian Wright, Penguin.

Upton Sinclair (1935) *We, People of America, and How We Ended Poverty*, EPIC Books.

Philip Slater (July 1, 1990) *The Pursuit of Loneliness*, 3rd edition, Beacon Press.

Matt Taibbi (2010) *Griftopia: A Story of Bankers, Politicians, and the Most Audacious Power Grab in American History* , Spiegel & Grau.

Alvin Toffler (1971) *Future Shock*, Bantam.

Harris Wofford, Jr. (1987) *Lohia and America Meet*, Sindhu Publications.

DOI: 10.1057/978-1-137-32516-7

# Index

*1984*, 88
2010 Commonwealth
   Games, 27
2G spectrum scam, 27
9/11, 9, 15, 80, 84

Adams, John, 64
Afghanistan, 6, 9, 36, 44, 63,
   95, 124
Ahmadis, 57
Al-Qaeda, 23, 125
Ambedkar, B. R., 71
America, 5, 10, 11, 14, 15, 17, 26,
   28, 30, 38, 46, 49, 67, 68, 78,
   81, 84, 86, 103, 106, 107, 110,
   123, 124, 126
Amir, Ayaz, 42
*Animal Farm*, 88
Annan, Kofi, 69
*Antyodaya*, 40
Arctic National Refuge, 45
Ashcroft, John, 81
assassination, 5, 10, 14, 21,
   118, 130
al-Awlaki, Anwar, 78, 87

Bacevich, Andrew, 113, 119
Badrinath, 36
Bageant, Joe, 33
bania, 60, 64
Belloc, Hilaire, 3, 107, 108
Berman, Morris, 128, 129, 131
*Bhagavad Gita*, 32, 41
*Bhoga Bhumi*, 45

Bin Laden, 81
Bizarro World, 15, 16
Blackwater, 29
Bose, Subhas Chandra, 70
Buchanan, Pat, 10
Buchman, Frank, 53
Buddha, 14, 44, 130
Bush, George W., 5, 41, 45, 46,
   79, 81, 87

CACI, 29
Caliphate, 87
Camus, Albert, 124, 131
Capitalism, 49
caste, 57, 59, 60, 62, 64, 93, 102
cell phone, 67
centralization, 112, 129
Chaudhuri, Nirad, 93
Chauri Chaura, 21, 22
Chesterton, G. K., 107, 108
child malnutrition, 61
China, 1, 3, 27, 29, 30, 31, 33, 38,
   49, 52, 66, 67, 68, 77, 81, 95
Chomsky, Noam, 77
Christ, 123
Churchill, Winston, 3
civil disobedience, 21, 22, 104
civilization, 3, 4, 30, 56, 57, 59,
   66, 124, 129
Civilization, 82, 107
*Clash of Civilizations, The*, 56, 63
class, 2, 17, 46, 49, 56, 58, 59,
   96, 111, 117
class struggle, 58, 59, 111

DOI: 10.1057/978-1-137-32516-7

climate change, 49
Cockburn, Alexander, 81, 92
Coke, Coca-Cola, 95, 97
colonialism, 21, 51
communism, 59, 60, 111, 115
Congress
    Indian National, 20
    US, 26, 45, 46, 56, 79
conscience, 21, 40, 86, 97, 106, 116
consciousness, 57, 58, 59, 114, 123
consumerism, 45, 52, 53, 92, 113
corruption, 18, 28, 30, 31, 34, 90, 91, 95,
    111, 112, 115, 118, 125
cottage industry, 9
cultural literacy, 80

Dar-ul Harb, 59
Dar-ul Islam, 59
Davos, 26
de Tocqueville, Alexis, 27
defense, 18, 44, 112, 117
democracy, 11, 28, 30, 62, 68, 72, 77,
    109, 113
development, 18, 36, 44, 45, 49, 50, 60,
    61, 73, 95, 126
Diamond, Jared, 66, 67
drug war, 10
Dyer, Gen. Reginald, 15, 23

Einstein, Albert, 128, 129
Eisenhower, Dwight, 112, 113, 117, 119, 120
elections, 9, 27, 30, 77, 88
Elitia, 41
Emerson, 5
empire, 62, 64
Enlightenment, 68, 73
environment, 30, 49, 50, 51, 63,
    122, 125
environmental, 2, 30, 50, 51, 53, 106,
    117, 126
environmentalist, 49
exports, 9, 37, 46

Facebook, 33
fear, 11, 14, 15, 17, 20, 50, 51, 69, 73, 76,
    86, 110, 111, 126, 129

fearlessness, 11
fertilizers, 51
Ford, Henry, 32, 49, 105
Franklin, Benjamin, 10
fundamentalist, 26, 49, 51

Gaddafi, Muammar, 61
gadgetry, 2, 67, 77, 81, 128
Gandhi, 50, 62, 87
Garrett, Garet, 62
GDP, 52, 67, 95
Ghalib, Mirza, 91, 102, 103, 104, 108
Gibran, Kahlil, 101, 108
Giraldi, Philip, 119
globalism, 39, 40, 41, 123
globalization, 35, 36, 37, 38, 39, 40, 41,
    42, 45, 52, 68, 86, 96, 123
Goebbels, Joseph, 88
Gorbachev, Mikhail, 86
Great Bengal Famine, the, 51
Great Trial of 1922, The, 106
greed, 4, 45, 50, 55, 60, 61, 62, 64, 114,
    123, 126, 127
Griftopia, 34
Grove, Andrew, 38, 42
growth rate, 26, 27, 30, 31, 32, 51, 52,
    92, 126
*Guide*, 19

*habeas corpus*, 23
*Harijan*, 64, 84, 99, 116, 119, 120, 131
Hazare, Anna, 91, 92
Hearst, William Randolph, 76
Himalayan. See Himalayas
Himalayas, 30, 36, 68
*Hind Swaraj*, 2, 3, 4, 5, 6, 22, 29, 32, 52,
    53, 54, 59, 60, 68, 71, 82, 104, 108,
    129, 131
Hindu, 23, 36, 57, 71, 93, 114
Hirsch, E. D., 80
Hitchcock, Alfred, 81
Hitler, Adolf, 15, 22
Hoffer, Eric, 21
Holmes, Sherlock, 27
Homeland Security, 118
Huntington, Samuel, 56, 58, 60, 63

DOI: 10.1057/978-1-137-32516-7

imports, 38, 61, 93
India, 1, 3, 4, 5, 8, 9, 11, 19, 20, 21, 23,
  24, 26, 27, 28, 29, 30, 31, 34, 36, 37, 38,
  39, 40, 41, 42, 44, 45, 46, 47, 49, 50,
  51, 52, 54, 57, 59, 60, 62, 63, 64, 66,
  67, 68, 71, 72, 73, 74, 82, 91, 92, 93, 95,
  96, 97, 99, 103, 104, 106, 107, 111, 112,
  113, 114, 115, 116, 117, 119, 120, 121, 126,
  127, 130
Industrial Revolution, 2, 9
industrialism, 51, 61, 101, 105, 107,
  119, 128
Iraq War, 46, 88
Islam, 16, 32, 53, 59, 63, 127
Israel, 59

Jallianwala Bagh, 23, 24, 70
Jaywalking, 79
Jefferson, Thomas, 11
Jinnah, M. A., 56, 57, 58
journalism, 5, 75, 82

Kallenbach, H., 129
Kanda, K. C., 93
Kapoor, Raj, 34
*Karma Bhumi*, 45
Kelly, Kathy, 86
Kennedy, John F., 46
*khadi*, 9, 93
Khan, Khan Abdul Ghaffar, 116, 120
King, Martin Luther, 11, 125
Kipling, Rudyard, 16, 36, 66
Kissinger, Henry, 80
Klein, Naomi, 24, 87, 110
Koestler, Arthur, 86
Kohr, Leopold, 32, 33
Korten, David, 52
Kunstler, James Howard, 106, 108

Lafayette, 42
Landes, David, 66, 68
Lenin, Vladimir, 15
Leno, Jay, 79
"Lesson from the Plague, A", 71
LeT, 19
liberalization, 92

liberation, 5, 41, 49, 50, 104, 105, 112
liberty, 8, 9, 10, 40, 117, 118
Limits to Growth, 52
Lind, William, 39, 42
locusts, 51
Lohia, Rammanohar, 11, 19, 23, 47, 57,
  59, 68, 69, 101, 114
LTTE, 23

Mahapatra, Sampad, 39
Mammon, 62
Mao, 34, 124
Maoist insurgency, 26
Marx, Karl, 11, 58, 111, 127
Marxism, 111
Marxist, 58, 59, 110
*Maxim Gun*, 3
media, 27, 76, 77, 78, 79, 81, 82, 83, 96,
  122, 124, 125
Meria, 39
military, 3, 16, 17, 18, 29, 31, 36, 46, 112,
  113, 117, 123, 127
Mohammad, Prophet, 123
Mohammed cartoons, 68
Monbiot, George, 38, 39, 81
monotony, 130
Monsanto, 92, 96
moral, 3, 10, 11, 16, 18, 19, 20, 35, 46, 47,
  58, 59, 63, 70, 85, 91, 103, 113, 114, 115,
  126, 127
Moynihan, Daniel Patrick, 56, 58
multiculturalism, 68
Muslim, 16, 60, 62, 63, 71

Nader, Ralph, 10, 77, 128
Nagler, Michael, 52
Naicker, Periyar E. V. Ramasami, 71
Naqvi, Jawed, 31, 34
Nasruddin, Mullah, 77, 78
Nazir Akbarabadi, 108
Nehru, Jawaharlal, 8, 9, 46, 47, 66, 82,
  84, 128, 130, 131
neoliberal, 34, 49, 92
Nero, 96
*New York Times*, 38, 77, 91
Nixon, Richard, 118

DOI: 10.1057/978-1-137-32516-7

nonviolence, 8, 9, 22, 70, 104
non-violent/nonviolent, 21, 112, 116
nuclear, 46, 50, 53, 125

Obama, Barack, 26, 27, 41, 78, 79, 118
Occupy movement, 106
oil, 10, 45, 61, 101
Orissa, 39, 40, 99
Orwell, George, 88

*paataala loka*, 114
Pakistan, 8, 11, 23, 36, 57, 59,
    62, 120
*Pandemonium*, 56
Patel, Aakar, 104, 108, 115, 120
Peacemaker, 53
Pepsi, 95
Piper, William, 39
Plachimada, 97
population, 4, 22, 53, 77, 79, 80,
    113, 115
POSCO, 39
Postman, Neil, 77
poverty, 40, 46, 58, 95, 98, 102
privatization, 26, 29, 30, 31, 33, 34
protectionism, 37
Punjab, 15, 23
Puri, 99
Putin, Vladimir, 87

Raimondo, Justin, 15, 16
rainforest, 4, 37, 52
Raj, the, 20, 24, 120
Rajagopalachari, C., 46, 64
Rall, Ted, 77, 84
Ramakrishnan, K. G., 46
Rand, Ayn, 11
Reagan, Ronald, 26, 78, 107, 118
Reed, Fred, 87
Rehnquist Supreme Court, 9
Rice, Condoleezza, 81
Roberts, Paul Craig, 78, 79, 118, 120
Romero, Lisa, 76
Rushdie, Salman, 69
Ruskin, John, 104, 105
Russell, Bertrand, 83, 123, 126

Sailer, Steve, 83
Sainath, P., 28, 95, 96, 97, 98
Samuelson, Paul, 38
Sanger, Margaret, 10
Sarvarkar, V. D., 56, 57, 58
Schumacher, E. F., 23, 63, 91, 93
self-restraint, 30, 61, 73, 83, 113,
    115, 122, 127
Sen, Amartya, 92
SEZ, 30
Shaw, George Bernard, 58, 59, 66, 73,
    107, 108, 127
Sheehan, Cindy, 86
Shia, 57
Sikh, 23
Silicon Valley, 8, 36
Singh, Bhagat, 19, 20, 21, 70
Singh, Manmohan, 8, 91, 92
Slater, Philip, 102
soil, 49, 51, 66, 99, 104
Solzhenitsyn, Aleksandr, 85, 86,
    87, 88, 118
Soviet Union, 1, 37, 86, 127
*SS Kildonan Castle*, 6
State
    actor, 23
    as antithesis of ahimsa, 111
    British state absent, 69
    changed focus, 27
    circumscribing power of the, 115
    and citizen as cog, 34
    civil disobedience as a check on
        the, 118
    combating terrorism, 17
    as congealed violence, 19
    connotation in political science, 110
    "daddy" and "nanny", 115
    "digital hive" a soft
    duty to foster economic growth,
        26
    fire sale of resources in Yeltsin
        era, 30
    and Gandhi on Bolshevism, 63
    Gandhi on state-made frontiers, 42
    and Gandhi's vision of
        Ramarajya, 115

DOI: 10.1057/978-1-137-32516-7

State – *continued*
    ideal response to terrorism, 24
    information from a paranoid, 76
    and legitimacy to use force, 111
    less intrusive, 19
    and liberalization, 30
    and Marxist theory, 110
    modernism and military-
        industrial, 113
    National Security State 2.0,
        87, 110
    not above party politics, 111
    as the populace, 114
    power in the
        ascendant, 109
    rampant post-9/11, 118
    rendered irrelevant, 114
    security and American
        freedoms, 110
    self-abnegation in US, 30
    Soviet, 110
    strengthening of, 112
    suborned to settle scores, 111
    tax holidays in India, 31
    terror, 19
    tool of corporate
        enrichment, 28
    totalitarian?, 33
    and trackable consumer, 33
    UN member-state savaged, 69
    and US taxes, 29
    violence and strategic
        inaction, 117
    withering away, 11, 110, 111
structural adjustment, 95, 97, 98
suicides
    farmer, 30, 92, 95, 98, 105
Sunni, 57

Swadeshi, 40, 41, 42
Swaraj, 8, 104, 130

Tagore, Rabindranath, 70, 103
Taliban, 44, 45, 125
taxes, 17, 28, 29, 38, 78, 91
technology, 2, 3, 33, 77, 81, 86, 87, 88,
    122, 124, 127
terrorism, 8, 14, 15, 17, 18, 19, 22,
    23, 24, 110
Thoreau, H. D., 104, 105
Toffler, Alvin, 1, 2
tolerance, 62, 69, 71, 73
Tolstoy, Leo, 14, 104, 105
trade, 8, 10, 37, 39, 46, 68, 73
Tripathi, Kamalapati, 88
Truth, 87
Twain, Mark, 4, 30, 58, 59, 127

*Uncle Tom's Cabin*, 101
United States. *See* America
untruth, 87, 88
US. *See* America

*Vaishnava Jana To*, 42
Vardhana, Ananda, 36
vegetarian, 50
violence, 9, 19, 20, 21, 22, 23, 55, 59, 88,
    109, 111, 116, 117

Werther, 81
Western civilization, 3, 4
Wodehouse, P. G., 105, 121

Yeltsin, Boris, 30, 86
Yervada Mandir, 84
*Young India*, 84
Yugoslavia, 56

DOI: 10.1057/978-1-137-32516-7

The manufacturer's authorised representative in the EU is Springer
Nature Customer Service Centre GmbH, Europaplatz 3, 69115 Heidelberg,
Germany. If you have any concerns regarding our products, please
contact ProductSafety@springernature.com

Printed and bound by CPI Group (UK) Ltd, Croydon, CR0 4YY
23/04/2026
02095587-0018